# TEXT AND PERFORMANCE

*General Editor:* Michael Scott

The series is designed to introduce sixth-form and under-graduate students to the themes, continuing vitality and performance of major dramatic works. The attention given to production aspects is an element of special importance, responding to the invigoration given to literary study by the work of leading contemporary critics.

The prime aim is to present each play as a vital experience in the mind of the reader – achieved by analysis of the text in relation to its themes and theatricality. Emphasis is accordingly placed on the relevance of the work to the modern reader and the world of today. At the same time, traditional views are presented and appraised, forming the basis from which a creative response to the text can develop.

In each volume, Part One: *Text* discusses certain key themes or problems, the reader being encouraged to gain a stronger perception both of the inherent character of the work and also of variations in interpreting it. Part Two: *Performance* examines the ways in which these themes or problems have been handled in modern productions, and the approaches and techniques employed to enhance the play's accessibility to modern audiences.

Synopses of the plays are given and reference is made to the commentaries of critics and other writers on the texts and performances. A concluding Reading List offers guidance to the student's independent study of the work.

PUBLISHED

| | |
|---|---|
| *Peer Gynt* and *Ghosts* | Asbjorn Aarseth |
| *The Duchess of Malfi* and | |
| *The White Devil* | Richard Cave |
| *Hamlet* | Peter Davison |
| *The Winter's Tale* | R. P. Draper |
| *The Crucible* and | |
| *Death of a Salesman* | Bernard Dukore |
| *Tamberlaine* and | |
| *Edward II* | George Geckle |
| *Volpone* | A. P. Hinchliffe |
| *The Tempest* | David L. Hirst |
| *The Birthday Party* and | |
| *The Caretaker* | Ronald Knowles |
| *Measure for Measure* | Graham Nicholls |
| *The Merchant of Venice* | Bill Overton |
| *Richard II* | Malcolm Page |
| *Twelfth Night* | Lois Potter |
| *King Lear* | Gāmini Salgādo |
| *Antony and Cleopatra* | Michael Scott |
| *Doctor Faustus* | William Tydeman |
| *Murder in the Cathedral* and | |
| *The Cocktail Party* | William Tydeman |
| *A Midsummer Night's Dream* | Roger Warren |
| *Henry the Fourth, Parts 1 and 2* | T. F. Wharton |
| *Macbeth* | Gordon Williams |
| *Othello* | Martin L. Wine |
| *Waiting for Godot* and | |
| *Happy Days* | Katharine Worth |

IN PREPARATION

| | |
|---|---|
| *The Real Thing* | Robert Gordon |
| *Much Ado About Nothing* | Pamela Mason |
| *Romeo and Juliet* | Peter Holding |

# WAITING FOR GODOT and HAPPY DAYS

## Text and Performance

### KATHARINE WORTH

**MACMILLAN**

First published 1990

Published by
MACMILLAN EDUCATION LTD
Houndmills, Basingstoke, Hampshire RG21 2XS
and London
Companies and representatives
throughout the world.

Printed in Hong Kong

British Library Cataloguing in Publication Data
Worth, Katharine
Waiting for Godot and Happy Days
—(Text and performance).
1. Drama in English. Beckett, Samuel, 1906– Critical studies
I. Title      II. Series
882'.9'2
ISBN 0–333–39578–6

# CONTENTS

*Happy Days*

# ACKNOWLEDGEMENTS

My grateful acknowledgements for permission to quote from *Waiting for Godot* and *Happy Days* are due to Samuel Beckett and to Faber and Faber, London, and Grove Press Inc., New York, A Division of Wheatland Corporation. I also wish to thank the Royal Exchange Theatre Company, Manchester for their generous help with information and illustrations.

# GENERAL EDITOR'S PREFACE

For many years a mutual suspicion existed between the theatre director and the literary critic of drama. Although in the first half of the century there were important exceptions, such was the rule. A radical change of attitude, however, has taken place over the last thirty years. Critics and directors now increasingly recognise the significance of each other's work and acknowledge their growing awareness of interdependence. Both interpret the same text, but do so according to their different situations and functions. Without the director, the designer and the actor, a play's existence is only partial. They revitalise the text with action, enabling the drama to live fully at each performance. The academic critic investigates the script to elucidate its textual problems, understand its conventions and discover how it operates. He may also propose his view of the work, expounding what he considers to be its significance.

Dramatic texts belong therefore to theatre and to literature. The aim of the 'Text and Performance' series is to achieve a fuller recognition of how both enhance our enjoyment of the play. Each volume follows the same basic pattern. Part One provides a critical introduction to the play under discussion, using the techniques and criteria of the literary critic in examining the manner in which the work operates through language, imagery and action. Part Two takes the enquiry further into the play's theatricality by focusing on selected productions of recent times so as to illustrate points of contrast and comparison in the interpretation of different directors and actors, and to demonstrate how the drama has worked on the modern stage. In this way the series seeks to provide a lively and informative introduction to major plays in their text and performance.

MICHAEL SCOTT

# INTRODUCTION

## 1 CHOICE OF PLAYS

The choice of *Waiting for Godot* for this volume needs little explanation. The first play of Beckett's to be performed (in Paris in 1953) it effected a revolution in the theatre, demolishing conventional ideas of plot and character and showing how a profound concern with the nature and meaning of human existence could be embodied in comedy which continually draws attention to itself as theatre and ironically undermines attempts to impose hard-and-fast meanings on it. Since Peter Hall directed the English version at the Arts Theatre in 1955, the theatre has absorbed Beckett in the way that Ibsen was once absorbed. *Waiting for Godot* has passed into the public consciousness: innumerable cartoons, jokes and stories testify to the assumption that even people who may never have read or seen the play will recognise the famous image of the two down-at-heel figures waiting by the tree for the Godot who never comes.

*Happy Days* (1961) has to face more competition, both from powerfully affecting early plays like *Endgame* (1957) and from the intense, very brief monologues of Beckett's later phase. *Happy Days,* however, has a claim to be the play of Beckett's which gives the richest portrayal of a single character. It is also the first of his plays to focus on a woman: apart from Nell in her dustbin in *Endgame* (a thin though crucial role), the casts in the first two stage plays were all male while this is a 'Female Solo' (Beckett's original working title for *Happy Days*). No doubt the success of the play in attracting actresses of great distinction to play the demanding part of Winnie encouraged Beckett to write more virtuoso female roles, as in *Not I* (1972), *Footfalls* (1976) and *Rockaby* (1981.) *Happy Days* is therefore the start of a new

line of character interest in Beckett's drama. It is also the
first of his plays to break completely with scenic realism.
For all these reasons, *Happy Days* is paired with *Waiting for
Godot* as a play of comparable substance and significance.

## 2  ENGLISH AND FRENCH VERSIONS

Beckett is unique in his practice of writing both in English
and French and in translating all his works himself from one
language to the other. With the translation thus guaranteed
by the author, the plays can fairly be studied as self-
contained works in either language. However, acquaintance
with the other language text is obviously desirable and can
be important.

The plays discussed in the volume fall rather neatly into
Beckettian pairs. *Waiting for Godot* was written in French as
*En attendant Godot*. At the time he wrote it (between October
1948 and January 1949) Beckett had been living in Paris for
years and was engaged on a massive trilogy of novels, all
written in French. He turned from the second of these,
*Malone meurt* (published like the first, *Molloy*, in 1951) to
write *En attendant Godot*. (The third novel, *L'innomable*, was
published in 1953.) It was thus natural for the first play he
had performed to be in French. *Happy Days*, on the other
hand, like almost all his plays after *Fin de partie* (*Endgame*),
was written first in English and then translated by Beckett
into French as *Oh les beaux jours*. His respect for Billie
Whitelaw's special ability to interpret such arduous roles as
Mouth must have been one element in this bias towards the
use of English in the theatre. But the bilingualism is always
in the background.

# PART ONE: TEXT

*Waiting for Godot*

### 3 NOTE ON THE TEXT

As *En attendant Godot*, the text was first published in 1952 (Paris: Les Editions de Minuit). Its first publication in English was in 1954 (New York: Grove Press). The first English edition was published in 1956: it has many minor variations from the American text and some bowdlerising, to meet the demands made by the Lord Chamberlain when the text was first staged in London.

The definitive edition of the English text was published by Faber and Faber (London, 1965) and is the text to which reference is made in this volume. (Note that the text included in *Samuel Beckett: the Complete Dramatic Works* (London: Faber and Faber, 1986) is the superseded text of 1956, not the edition of 1965.) Beckett has since revised the play as a result of directing it. A 'performance text' edition of the English version, edited by Dougald McMillan and James Knowlson, is in preparation. It will be published by Faber and Faber and Grove Press (New York), in a series under the general editorship of James Knowlson, with *Krapp's Last Tape*, edited by James Knowlson and *Endgame*, edited by Stanley Gontarski.

### 4 THE SITUATION

It is evening on a country road. Vladimir and Estragon (nicknames, Didi and Gogo) invent ways to pass the time while waiting by the solitary tree they think may be their trysting place with the Mr Godot whom they have never met. They have nothing else to do. Turning that nothing into something is their business, and they work at it throughout the two acts of the play with little help except from their own wit and each other. Twice in each act 'reinforcements' arrive. In the first act tyrannical Pozzo, driving Lucky by a rope, creates a grotesque performance for the benefit of the other two, forcing his decrepit slave to dance and then 'think'. In the second act the yoked couple reappear, on a shorter rope which Pozzo now needs because he has become blind (and Lucky dumb). Towards the close of each act a Boy appears with a message from Godot: he cannot come that day but will be there without fail the next. At the end of their tether, Vladimir and Estragon contemplate hanging themselves from the trysting tree but the idea breaks up in farcical confusion. Like the first act, the second ends with one of them suggesting 'Let's go', and neither moving.

## 5  STRUCTURE AND SETTING

Even so curt an outline of the plot may perhaps indicate that symmetry is one of the most striking features of the play. The impression of a random, inconsequential, even shapeless action which baffled early audiences is an artful illusion designed to draw the audience into the feelings Vladimir and Estragon have about the slow passage of time, the perpetual threat of boredom, the sense that existence may be a void in which there is no special reason for being anywhere or doing anything in particular. But the shape of the action contradicts the idea of shapelessness that bothers the characters. Everything is symmetrical and tends to come in doubles.

One inseparable couple is matched by another, equally though more miserably interdependent. In each act a Boy appears; each time he fails to remember having met Vladimir and Estragon before but repeats the same message, that Godot will come tomorrow. In each act there is a performance within the performance; Lucky dances and 'thinks'; Vladimir and Estragon, casting around for occupation when on their own in the second act, 'do' Pozzo and Lucky and Estragon tries to 'do' the tree. In each act Vladimir and Estragon contemplate suicide, getting somewhat further with the idea in the second act but ending as they were in the first act, talking about going but not going.

There is, too, a persistent emphasis on visual symmetry. The setting represents bare space, broken by one permanent scenic feature, the tree. Beckett's laconic direction – '*A country road. A tree. Evening.*' – leaves a certain amount of room for variation, which designers have exploited in varying degrees, but his own emphasis is on the innerness of the landscape. In later plays, like *Not I*, with its livid Mouth floating in stage darkness, we can tell from a reading of the text alone that the setting is some psychic space or void, a 'soul-landscape'. This is not so clear from the textual directions in *Waiting for Godot*, though Beckett has made his own view apparent in the Production Notebook he kept while directing the play with the Schiller-Theater, West Berlin, in 1975. James Knowlson has drawn attention to the emphasis he gives in it to the idea of imprisonment. At one point Beckett was thinking of having the faint shadow of bars cast on the stage floor, pointing up the symbolism of the space in which Vladimir and Estragon are, as he put it, 'two caged dynamics'.[1]

Only two set changes are specified in the text. Both open up a faint hope of relief for the characters from their oppressive consciousness of arid, empty space. 'At last!' says Vladimir when at the end of Act 2 a moon appears, with startling suddenness, as it had done in Act 1 at exactly the same point, following the exit of the Boy. The moon promises night and sleep, a respite from troubling thoughts such as those the Boy's appearance stimulates about the enigma of Godot. And between Acts 1 and 2 there is another startling change: the tree acquires leaves, though optimistic Vladimir exaggerates when he says it is 'covered' with them.

The wry stage direction [p. 57] suggests *'four or five'*. The meaning of this unnaturally swift leafing is uncertain, like so much else in the play, but it has one sure effect: it keeps the tree a centre of attention and speculation. For Vladimir, who broods on the possibility of divine interventions, the leafing seems a near-miracle. 'But yesterday evening it was all black and bare' he insists to the unimpressed Estragon, 'And now it's covered with leaves' [p. 66]. Estragon remains unimpressed. There is a natural explanation: 'It must be the Spring'. Or they are not in the same place as yesterday. How can one tell, when time has ceased to matter and memory has rejected these divisions? Beckett reminds us too, through the overt artificiality of his amusing *'four or five'*, that the mysterious change is after all contrived by the stage management, literally between the acts.

Beckett gets a great deal from those few leaves! And so with the tree itself: its symbolism may be more obvious in performance but the text suggests clearly that the simple visual image carries worlds of complex thought. It can stand for Spring, as Estragon comments; for renewals, therefore, and the cycle of life. Yet it is also associated with death, since the two plan to hang themselves from it. At that point it may connect in our minds with the Crucifixion, the 'tree' from which Christ hung; the text never lets us forget that event. But all options are open, including the possibility that all speculation is only part of a great illusion. It is a loaded joke indeed when Vladimir, failing to find refuge behind the tree from what seems like an approaching invasion (in fact Pozzo and Lucky), declares, 'Decidedly this tree will not have been of the slightest use to us' [p. 74].

## 6   RHYTHM, LANGUAGE AND STYLE

One of the most extraordinary aspects of the play is its rhythm. Even in reading it to ourselves, the text slows us down, by its pauses, its repetitions, its circularities. Time is slowed down to a crawl in the intervals of the brisk little conversational 'canters' which Vladimir and Estragon devise. 'This is becoming really insignificant' says Vladimir, after one of these. 'Not enough' is Estragon's reply. The object seems to be to get the action down to zero; that, or get off the stage for good, neither of which aims they can achieve. At times this dream-like rhythm becomes more markedly musical, as in the sequence beginning 'All the dead voices' where melodious phrases move in and out of silences, mimicking the ghostly sounds of the dead, as Vladimir and Estragon imagine them:

| | |
|---|---|
| VLADIMIR: | They make a noise like feathers. |
| ESTRAGON: | Like leaves. |
| VLADIMIR: | Like ashes. |
| ESTRAGON: | Like leaves. |
| | *Long silence.* |

[p. 63]

These quiet moments are contrasted, however, with bursts of noisier action where the rhythm speeds up, as in Lucky's nonstop 'think' [pp. 42–5] or the staccato duel of insults [p. 75].

The language of the play is at times deceptively simple. Little words arranged in seemingly artless fashion gather force by repetition and rhythmic emphasis, as in the most famous of all, the recurring interchange between Vladimir and Estagon:

| | |
|---|---|
| ESTRAGON: | . . . Let's go. |
| VLADIMIR: | We can't. |
| ESTRAGON: | Why not? |
| VLADIMIR: | We're waiting for Godot. |
| ESTRAGON: | (*despairingly*) Ah! . . . . |

[p. 14]

Without a single word of special note, this passage acquires increased power each time it appears. The full force and meaning of the language are conveyed to an unusual degree through tone, rhythm, repetition. We need to be on the alert for the seriousness implicit in simple words, for example

the word 'Help' which is heard throughout. Estragon asks
for help with his boots, Pozzo for help in getting off the
ground. Neither occasion would seem potentially tragic
without the insistent repetition that reminds us of the
human propensity to disregard or minimise the pain of
others. The idea is launched at the start in the conversation
[p. 10] about painful boots which provokes Vladimir into
the angry remark, 'No one ever suffers but you. I don't
count'. Close reading of the text reveals many minute and
significant changes of phrasing, as when Estragon, towards
the end, volunteers a statement in the first person about
what he is doing there: 'I'm waiting for Godot'.

Contrasts and shifts of tone continually hint at the
genuineness or otherwise of what is being said. It is obvious
for most of the time, for instance, that there is a vast
linguistic gap between Pozzo and the other pair. Pozzo's
melodramatics and literary affectations make him seem to
be always posturing and speechifying, sometimes absurdly,
as when he bemoans the loss of his watch — 'Twas my
granpa gave it to me!' — or brings out an intermittently
'lyrical' tone for his set-piece on the twilight [pp. 37–8]. Yet
there are times when the text may leave us less sure about
what is intended. Beckett's stage direction '*lyrically*' is
usually a warning of something pretentious to follow, but
some of Pozzo's speeches introduced in that way have been
taken seriously, when he holds forth on human misery, for
instance: 'The tears of the world are a constant quantity' [p.
33].

It is easier to see where we are with Vladimir and
Estragon, their spare, colloquial mode of speech being so
much closer to what we think of as natural (though wit like
theirs doesn't grow on every tree). But there is no less need
for alertness in following their dialogue if we are to register
all the shifts of tone which the witty pair have at their
command. Their linguistic repertoire ranges from everyday
colloquialisms, slang and dry jokes to Biblical allusions,
literary quotations and rhetoric, though of a very different
kind from Pozzo's. We cannot doubt that it is serious when
in Act 2 Vladimir looks down at the sleeping Estragon and
begins a long, brooding soliloquy with the troubled ques-

tion, 'Was I sleeping while the others suffered? Am I sleeping now?' The lines ring true in the same way as the banter between the two which suggests that for all their differences they are essentially on the same wavelength. They use a relaxed kind of shorthand much of the time, picking up each others' ideas for 'canters' with ease. They show a sly awareness of their bilingual origins:

| | |
|---|---|
| ESTRAGON: | Que voulez-vous? |
| VLADIMIR: | I beg your pardon? |
| ESTRAGON: | Que voulez-vous? |
| VLADIMIR: | Ah! que voulez-vous? Exactly. |

[p. 65]

With similar ease the pair move into Irish idiom: 'It was Lucky gave it to you'; 'Ah stop blathering and help me off with this bloody thing'. Their dialogue is full of literary echoes, though the quotations are often left unfinished (a sure way of drawing attention to them) as in Vladimir's 'Hope deferred maketh the something sick, who said that?' We may or may not know that the saying comes from *Proverbs* or that it finishes, 'But when the desire comes it is a tree of life' (another covert allusion to the hopeful aspect of the stage tree). We may be expected, however, to supply the missing word 'heart'. Vladimir is 'heart sick' waiting for Godot: how sentimental and Pozzo-like it might seem if said without the protection of a joke. The dialogue continually balances on this fragile line between humour and deep, sad feeling.

Behind the wonderful simplicities as well as the elaborations of the language lies a wealth of poetry and learning which is sometimes parodied, as in Pozzo's pompous rhetoric and — most fantastically — in Lucky's 'think'. His grotesque outpourings reduce learned language and style to absurdity: '. . . as a result of the labours left unfinished crowned by the Acacacacademy of Anthropopopometry of Essy-in-Possy . . . .' [p.43]. Substitute the Latin 'Esse' for 'Essy' and so on, and the outlines of a legalistic kind of philosophic debate on the existence of God appear. The language is learned, rich in latinisms, some obscure, like

'succedanea', some legalistic, punctuated horrifically at the
start with the 'quaquaquaqua' that makes nonsense of it as
it goes along. The think is not all parody, however. Poetic
words like 'waste' and 'pine' thrust their way forward, in
comically uneasy relation to more ordinary words to do with
'sports of all sorts'. Men are unable to fill their minds, the
incoherent speech suggests, with 'golf over nine and
eighteen holes tennis of all sorts . . . in Feckham Peckham
Fulham Clapham'. Tennis competes to the end with the
language of wasting and pining and dwindling.. The speech
has no punctuation; it is jumbled, spasmodic and it ends on
the word 'unfinished', so we do not look for coherence or
conclusions. But still, leitmotifs assert themselves; the
'skull in Connemara' looms out at us, a troubling image that
cannot be covered up by any amount of distracting words.
This is one of the places in the text where we must feel most
curious to know how the sound of the words and the look of
the actor delivering them will affect interpretation. Beckett
himself gave a large clue when he marked in his Schiller-
Theater Notebook three divisions to the speech: 'Indifferent
heaven; Dwindling man; Earth abode of stones — cadenza'.
Our curiosity should extend to the whole text, however, for
it is a text which demands to be voiced. Intonation, shifts of
tone and mood, grouping, movement are all woven together
to create the 'shape' which is the play's deepest meaning.

## 7  THE PAIRS

*Vladimir and Estragon*

The inseparable, ill-assorted but mutually dependent couple is a favourite subject with Beckett. Vladimir and
Estragon had predecessors in the early novel, *Mercier et
Camier* (written in 1946, two years before *Godot*, though not
published till 1970). Mercier and Camier are contrasted,
complementary and at times it seems interchangeable

beings, a 'pseudocouple', to use Beckett's own word. Their
narrator comments drily at one point: 'Mercier, up to now,
had shown himself the live wire, Camier the dead weight.
The reverse was to be expected at any moment'. Reversals
of a similar kind occur between Vladimir and Estragon.
They are contrasted, and sometimes switched, in the age-
old style of comic turns that draw fun from physical
disparities: Stan Laurel, cadaverously lean, Oliver Hardy
short and fat, for instance, making up the familiar,
inseparable image we think of as Laurel and Hardy.

On seeing the first performance of *Waiting for Godot* in
Paris, Jean Anouilh brilliantly described this disconcerting
fusion of frivolous and profound as a 'music-hall sketch of
Pascal's *Pensées* played by the Fratellini clowns'. 'Pensées' or
thoughts are certainly what Vladimir and Estragon play
with, and the emphasis must be on play, but the feeling of
the players is bound up in the game in a very serious way. It
is typical, for instance, in the opening sequence, that for no
apparent reason and not in response to anything Estragon
has said, Vladimir should come out with an oblique
reference to Christ's supposed words on the cross to the two
thieves who were crucified with him. One moment he and
Estragon are discussing the latter's trouble with his feet, the
next, Vladimir is examining the inside of his hat ('This is
getting alarming') and then after a silence in which he is
'deep in thought', he suddenly comes out with the cryptic
comment: 'One of the thieves was saved. (*Pause.*) It's a
reasonable percentage' [p. 11]. The effect is inconsequential but it is the sort of inconsequentiality that tells us a lot
about Vladimir's mind: his brooding nature, his preoccupation with the Christian story and its messages about
salvation and damnation.

The routines and turns at their seemingly most random
or inconsequential in fact continually lead into speculations
on the oddity of language or of thought or on the nature of
things. In Act 1, for instance [pp. 20–21], a regular 'turn' on
carrots and turnips begins with the broad comic business of
Vladimir handing Estragon a turnip when he asks for a
carrot but leads into exchanges that, although keeping the
light, even frolicsome touch, are also probing and reflective:

| | |
|---|---|
| ESTRAGON: | Fancy that. (*He raises what remains of the carrot by the stub of leaf, twirls it before his eyes.*) Funny, the more you eat the worse it gets. |
| VLADIMIR: | With me it's just the opposite. |
| ESTRAGON: | In other words? |
| VLADIMIR: | I get used to the muck as I go along. |
| ESTRAGON: | (*after prolonged reflection*). Is that the opposite? |
| VLADIMIR: | Question of temperament. |
| ESTRAGON: | Of character. |
| VLADIMIR: | Nothing you can do about it. |
| ESTRAGON: | No use struggling. |
| VLADIMIR: | One is what one is. |
| ESTRAGON: | No use wriggling. |
| VLADIMIR: | The essential doesn't change. |
| ESTRAGON: | Nothing to be done. (*He proffers the remains of the carrot to Vladimir.*) Like to finish it? |

[p. 21]

The trivial business, it turns out, is not trivial viewed from the perspective human thought imposes on it. So with the physical condition of the pair. This is subject for wry mirth, as always in the world of the clown. Estragon enjoys as a bit of a show Vladimir's precipitate exits on account of his urinary trouble, calling to Pozzo on one occasion to take a look off-stage at the 'performance'. Pozzo puts on his glasses to see better, exclaiming 'Oh I say!'. And Vladimir gets a joke out of Estragon's complaints about his ill-fitting boot and his plea for help: 'There's man all over for you, blaming on his boots the fault of his feet'.

Yet these dilapidations are also bleak: symptoms of mortality, a reminder of the inevitable decay of the human body. It is very ordinary suffering and that is the point. Vladimir and Estragon can easily be recognised as representatives of the human race, coping with the ills the flesh is heir to, as well as other more intangible anxieties. They are in their way tragic heroes, raising pity and terror (the classical outcome of tragedy) as well as amusement and thought. We might recall that Beckett has called the play (in the English, not the original French version) a tragicomedy. There is something heroic in the ability of these two down-at-heel characters to surmount their troubles, especially as the troubles so clearly are going to be endlessly with them. Everything returns and repeats, a point made at the opening of Act 2 when Vladimir sings the 'dog song', the song that goes round in circles.

Estragon also has more violent experience of physical pain. He spends his nights separate from Vladimir and at the beginning of each act is questioned by his friend about another kind of familiar ordeal, the nightmare: 'Who beat you? Tell me.' Refusal to reply hints at traumatic happenings: 'Don't touch me! Don't question me! Don't speak to me! Stay with me!'. It may be that in the background was the horror of the Nazis' regime and its impact on people close to Beckett when the Germans occupied France. He himself, with his wife, was a member of the French Resistance; they escaped the Gestapo by a hair's breadth and experienced much hardship in the rural area of Vichy France where they took refuge. It would be surprising if this grim experience were not reflected in the play. Estragon was originally to have been called Lévy, which would have been a clear link with the suffering of that time, and the name Estragon also points that way with its phonic closeness to tarragon, a bitter herb.

As with everything to do with this pair, dark and light are mixed in kindly and fundamentally tender ways. They bicker, get on each other's nerves and talk about parting but their affection always survives. Vladimir takes a protective role, poignantly seen in Act 2 when he places his coat over the shoulders of his sleeping friend, who finds sleep difficult. Characteristically, Estragon wakes violently from this sleep which has turned into one of his nightmares. And characteristically Vladimir comforts him.

Vladimir and Estragon are opposites who complement each other. Estragon is the more emotional — uninhibited, capricious and on occasion violent. He has a highly selective memory and he is also the dreamer and poet, appropriately shabby to prove it, as he comments with typical tart feeling. Vladimir is the inventive thinker who pursues reasonable explanations, tries to bring dark things into the light of day, and is more fully turned to the world of others than Estragon. But just when we may think they have divided themselves on opposite sides of a line, they will reveal how much they have in common. Vladimir, the man of reason, is obsessively preoccupied with the mystery of the Crucifixion and that faint promise of salvation for *one* of the thieves. Estragon on the other hand professes to have small knowledge of the Bible in Act 1 ('I must have taken a look at it'). Yet in Act 2, on entering barefoot, he declares that all his life he has compared himself to Christ.

We are likely to be struck by the idea that these two separate characters are really to be thought of as elements in one personality, a more complex and humanised version of the mind/body split speculated on by philosophers like Descartes (and by Beckett himself, in his early fiction). Something of the sort is seen on the stage of W. B. Yeats, a writer very important to Beckett. Similar thoughts may occur when the second pair enter the scene.


*Pozzo and Lucky*


On the face of it, the relationship of Pozzo and Lucky is altogether simpler than that of the other pair, besides being obviously more unpleasant. When they first erupt on to the stage, Lucky loaded with impedimenta he can only put down on command, driven by Pozzo on the end of a long rope which makes a running sore on his neck, the image is unequivocally one of master and slave. These two are indeed tied, as Estragon had wondered whether he and Vladimir were tied (to Godot). They also present a more violent contrast of character, perhaps along the line of Ruby Cohn's 'mental versus physical man'.[2] Pozzo is certainly grossly physical, preoccupied with his comforts and capable of feasting 'voraciously' on chicken and wine without the least thought of offering a share to any of the three who stand around, watching hungrily.

In fierce contrast, Lucky is a miserable figure, unable even to think without an order — and when his hat is on his head. The mention of hats, however, must pull us up a moment. Beckett puts great emphasis on the ubiquitous nature of these bowler hats which get passed around,

swapped, trampled on in the course of the play. When
Vladimir and Estragon pick up Lucky's abandoned hat and
play games with it, they might be thought of as entering into
some strange, composite identity in which each pair
represents a different psychic arrangement: they are alien
and yet in touch. Certainly they share rather more than
bowler hats. In their so different ways each pair is
committed to a purpose which is seen as giving meaning to
their existence. Pozzo's is to continue on the road from
which he has come, following a clear-cut time scheme (the
line of history perhaps). For Vladimir and Estragon the
purpose is equally clear (though hardly understood): they
are waiting for Godot. Parallels can be multiplied. In each
pair or set the two elements are tied, more brutally in one,
but not more certainly. And in each there is both contrast
and affinity between the personae who are yoked together.
The possibility of the pairs drawing closer together, despite
the chasm between them, is subtly insinuated in the first
act: in the second act it is realised, for it is not altogether
ironical when Pozzo in extremity is described by Vladimir
as 'all humanity'.

At first, or course, the focus is on the startling contrast
between Vladimir/Estragon and Pozzo/Lucky, a contrast so
powerful that the couples almost appear to inhabit two
separate worlds. Their different sense of time is one of the
great dividers. As Bert States puts it, they 'dramatise
antithetical concepts of being-in-time'.[3] One pair feel
themselves in a 'void' where 'time has stopped' and life goes
round in circles. The other two cut through the void,
seemingly unaware of it, following the straight line dictated
by chronology. Pozzo is intensely time-conscious: he makes
great play with his watch, 'cuddling' it to his ear when
Vladimir pronounces 'Time has stopped' and protesting,
'Don't you believe it, sir, don't you believe it . . . Whatever
you like, but not that' [p. 36]. In Act 2, however, as a blind
man, he has no use for watches. 'Have you not done tormenting me with your accursed time!' [p. 89] he bursts out when
Vladimir persists in his questions as to *when* blindness
struck him (and Lucky went dumb). This is one of the
strange, drastic changes which in the second act push the

personae into the position of 'the other', a process which
can be seen as movement away from habit, the 'deadener',
into what Beckett has called 'the suffering of being'.[4]

Contradictions, disconcerting twists and turns are part of
Beckett's technique for maintaining a suggestive ambiguity
about the connectedness or otherwise of the separate
personae and of the pairs. Pozzo provides the most
spectacular example of the instability to which all are
subject. He is probably the character whose lines have
received most revision in Beckett's rewriting of the play, a
process to be noted later. (The discussion that follows is
based on the current text.) He is a mass of contradictions.
Tyrannical, confident, self-satisfied, he is also childishly
dependent, nervous and helpless, unable even to sit down
on occasion without a signal from outside:

| | |
|---|---|
| ESTRAGON: | Come come, take a seat, I beseech you, you'll get pneumonia. |
| POZZO: | You really think so? |
| ESTRAGON: | Why it's absolutely certain. |
| POZZO: | No doubt you are right. (*He sits down.*) Done it again! |

[p. 36]

Pozzo has arranged this game of make-believe into which
Estragon so obligingly enters. He knows he cannot move of
his own initiative at that point — as he can never do
anything without the assistance of his menial. He seems
always to be engaged in a kind of make-believe, protecting
himself with exaggerated flourishes, as when he roars with
laughter at the idea of Vladimir and Estragon being his
fellows:

Of the same species as myself. (*He bursts into an enormous
laugh.*)
Of the same species as Pozzo! Made in God's image!

[p. 23]

This little trick of referring to himself in the third person —
'the same species as Pozzo' — highlights the self-centred-
ness and self-dramatising which has led to his being seen as

an embodiment of the ego. It is a symbolic role that fits him quite easily, more snugly than that of the will which has also been assigned to him by criticism. No simple connections with abstract concepts like will and ego can be made to work — the personae are too mercurial — but we can scarcely avoid thinking in symbolic terms about Pozzo and his relationship with Lucky. The fantastical nature of their presentation invites it. And from such an angle Pozzo seems to represent something deep in the human animal, an ego-centred force that is both alarming and absurd.

He is absurd in the way of an old-fashioned actor, a real ham, always looking for an audience (like his successor who is actually called Hamm in *Endgame*). Vladimir and Estragon play audience to him: they are normally performers themselves, so this is a change of role to be enjoyed in the endless performance they sometimes feel their life to be. What Pozzo gives them when he settles down to explain the twilight is a dismal sample of his powers, creaking between the utterly prosaic and an affected lyricism, as Beckett stresses in his stage directions:

> (*Lyrical.*) An hour ago (*he looks at his watch, prosaic*) roughly (*lyrical*) after having poured forth ever since (*he hesitates, prosaic*) say ten o'clock in the morning (*lyrical*) tirelessly torrents of red and white light it begins to lose its effulgence, to grow pale....
>
> [p. 37]

Is this the speech-maker on a bad day or is Pozzo incapable of true imaginative effort? Is everything about him phoney except the material possessions by which he projects himself, the watch, the throat spray, the whip? It is almost impossible to tell in Act 1, for he swings so unnervingly between different elements of his unstable personality. He appears totally lacking in self-criticism, quite missing the tongue-in-cheek style of his audience's response to his request for a rating of his performance — Vladimir's 'Oh very good, very very good', followed by Estragon's mocking 'Oh tray bong, tray tray tray bong'. 'Bless you, gentlemen, bless you!' he says, and 'I have such need of encourage-

ment!' [p. 38]. This is absurd indeed: it must make us
wonder whether he can be taken seriously at all, though we
have only to look at his slave on the end of the rope, or hear
Pozzo speaking in a different tone (as in the grim 'He
refused once') to know that we cannot afford to discount his
power, over men as well as things.

In the second act a remarkable change has occurred in
Pozzo's style as well as his circumstances. He still keeps his
sense of being on a stage, asking if this is the place 'known as
the Board?', a phrase usually taken to refer to the old idiom
for the stage, 'the boards'. But he has little of the histrionic
zest of Act 1, spending most of the time collapsed on the
ground, unable to get up without a helping hand from
Vladimir and Estragon. His rhetoric is cut almost to
nothing. When it comes, however, it is far removed from the
affected speechifying of the first act. Goaded by intrusive
talk of 'time', he utters a speech we do not feel inclined to
laugh at. Critics have given it much weight:

> . . . one day he went dumb, one day I went blind, one day
> we'll go deaf, one day we were born, one day we shall die, the
> same day, the same second, is that not enough for you?
> (*Calmer.*) They give birth astride of a grave, the light gleams
> an instant, then it's night once more.
>
> [p. 89]

Pozzo has become a more serious character, it seems,
because he suffers. 'Do I look like a man that can be made to
suffer?' he had asked in Act 1. Then we should surely have
had to say 'No'. But now the case is altered. These
movements towards true feeling are part of the still stranger
movement of all four disparate personae into the same zone
of being. As ever, the process is represented in half-comic
terms. First one pair fall down and call for help; then, after a
long wait for reflection, the other pair respond, and fall
down themselves. For a moment all are collapsed in a heap,
seemingly incapable of rising of their own accord. It is the
'fall of man', we may suppose, taking up the hints scattered
in the many biblical allusions that link the characters with
the Christian doctrines of fall and redemption and Old

Testament analogues. While Pozzo and Lucky lie in an inchoate mass, Vladimir tries calling out the name 'Abel'. Pozzo at once responds with a further cry for help. 'Perhaps the other is called Cain,' suggests Estragon, referring to Lucky. But when 'Cain' is called, Pozzo again responds, drawing from Estragon the significant remark, 'He's all humanity' [p. 83].

The surprising idea of Pozzo as Abel and Lucky as Cain leads into the question: who is tormenting whom? Lucky has the goitre caused by the rope to prove he is a victim but in Act 1 Pozzo claims that it is the other way round, it is Lucky who makes *him* suffer:

> I can't bear it . . . any longer . . . the way he goes on . . . you've no idea . . . it's terrible . . . he must go . . . (*he waves his arms*) . . . I'm going mad . . . (*he collapses, his head in his hands*) . . . I can't bear it . . . any longer . . .
>
> [p. 34]

He immediately contradicts himself: 'you may be sure there wasn't a word of truth in it'. So we are left unsure what to think, in other words, in the classical situation of the play. Uncertainty rules . . . The questions that cluster round the abject figure of Lucky are among the most puzzling in the play. He is the only one who doesn't speak for himself; he can't express a thought without a command from Pozzo — 'Think!' — and can't answer back or explain himself. In the second act he has lost his power of speech altogether, in line with the diminishing process that affects everything (the act is shorter, the Pozzo/Lucky episode briefer and so on). Pozzo has to 'represent' Lucky for us; the Lucky that once was, the 'good angel' we are never going to see, who bestowed 'beautiful things' on his master — 'Beauty, grace, truth of the first water' [p. 33]. Can we believe this? Would Pozzo even recognise such things? Or, if there was once such a teaching, what went wrong?

If we do give credence to Pozzo, Lucky becomes, rather strangely, a kind of 'fallen angel' turned 'wicked', the word Pozzo uses to warn Vladimir against going too near him [p. 22]. He is certainly 'fallen', being capable of the same bad

tendencies as everyone else in the play. Given the chance,
he too turns aggressor, kicking Estragon violently on the
shin when the latter tries to wipe away his tears. Why is he
called Lucky? The passage on p. 27 has suggested to some
critics that it is because he gets the bones; others follow
Beckett in surmising that it may be because he has nothing
left to hope for, a grim kind of luck. One puzzling question
is pursued by Estragon over six pages [pp. 25–31]: 'Why
doesn't he put down his bags?'. Pozzo's answer, when it
comes, again insists on Lucky's autonomy: he is free to put
them down but chooses not to. Why not? Pozzo produces an
explanation — 'He wants to impress me, so that I'll keep
him' — but he has to reword it, apparently to convince
himself, and finally remains uncertain: 'Well, that's what I
think'. These doubts and hesitations help to maintain the
separateness of the personae: they are not totally knowable
to each other.

Cross-connections have also been made by commentators
linking Vladimir with Lucky and Estragon with Pozzo:
intellect and physical being. The first is easier to argue than
the second. It is certainly Vladimir, the more intellectual of
the first pair, who puts Lucky's hat on his head in order to
hear him 'think', and who peers curiously into it after
snatching it off to stop him thinking. The affinities cannot
be pressed too far but cannot be ruled out. So too with the
idea of an artistic partnership between Pozzo and Lucky
which has been deduced from their dependence on each
other for expression in performance.

What manner of performance Lucky's really is cannot be
resolved fully from the text. No clue is given as to the nature
of his dance: the stage direction is simply (*Lucky dances*). We
may deduce that it is not up to much from Estragon's 'Pooh!
I'd do as well myself', though we should note that when he
tries to prove his claim by imitating Lucky's steps, he
almost falls [p. 40]. Interpretations from the stage audience
there are in plenty. Interestingly, it is Pozzo who supplies
the one nearest to Beckett's own idea, 'The Net. He thinks
he's entangled in a net'. How the actor playing Lucky
actually renders the dance is a question we must be
particularly curious to see answered in performance. The

same is obviously true of the think. If Lucky stands for some
form of intellect, he is parodying himself in the pedantry
and false logic of his discussion of the nature of God. False,
because it begins with an absurd claim to have been proved:
'Given the existence as uttered forth in the public works of
Puncher and Wattmann of a personal God quaquaquaqua. . .'
[p. 42]. But he cannot be thought of as representing only the
break-down or futility of logic when confronting such
mysteries. The speech is appalling as an intellectual
exercise in its runaway incoherence, its jumble of ideas, its
moments of absurd pedantry: 'the dead loss per caput since
the death of Bishop Berkeley being to the tune of one inch
four ounce per caput'. Still, it makes its way toward a
genuine lamentation over the sadness of human existence,
no less poignant or disturbing for proceeding from so
wretched a source. It might indeed be said that the beggarly
nature of the speaker adds force to his confused but
fearsome vision of humanity in extremity: 'the great cold
the great dark the air and the earth abode of stones in the
great cold. . .'.

## Godot and the Boy

Where in the text would we look for Godot? The answer to
that question takes us to the heart of the play and is known
even to people who have never read or seen it. He is
nowhere and everywhere; the one who will never come and
the one whose coming is always expected. Beckett once
thought of giving him more apparent solidity by having
Vladimir read to Estragon a letter making the appointment
by the tree. All that remains of the idea is Vladimir's
attempt to check that they have the right day by feeling in
his pocket ('I must have made a note of it') after Estragon's
sceptical questioning [p. 15]. Time and place for the
rendezvous can never be verified, as their first conversation
on the subject hints clearly:

VLADIMIR:        .... What are you insinuating? That we've
                come to the wrong place?

| ESTRAGON: | He should be here. |
| VLADIMIR: | He didn't say for sure he'd come. |
| ESTRAGON: | And if he doesn't come? |
| VLADIMIR: | We'll come back tomorrow. |

[p. 14]

The exchange draws from Vladimir the impatient, 'Nothing is certain when you're about', a line which might be said to express the ruling motif of the play.

Godot exists in that the play would not exist without him. The fact that he does not appear makes him no less a possibility: the off-stage character whom everyone talks and thinks about but who never shows up can acquire an extraordinary reality, a fact demonstrated across the whole range of drama, from light comedies like Gerald Savory's *George and Margaret* to the Greek tragedies in which invisible gods activate events by remote control. Godot exists in both the comedy of Beckett's play and its more tragic sphere: in relation to him, as to everything else, comedy and tragedy cannot be separated. The pair at one moment will allow themselves (under guard of flippancy) the language of tragedy: they have made 'supplication' to Godot, a 'kind of prayer' [p. 18]. In the next breath that is all swept away by reductive irony: his failure to respond is no more than happens in the ordinary world of 'agents' and 'bank accounts'.

What is meant by Godot is the question the play plants deep in our consciousness. Much has been written to deny that God was what Beckett had in mind. (The phonic closeness of 'Godot' to 'God' exists only for English audiences.) These caveats are valuable if they prevent attempts to allegorise in an over-simple way. The one thing we can be sure of is that we cannot be sure: 'Nothing is certain'. The vast variety of interpretations that have been offered suggests that Godot can stand for almost anything that keeps people going, their lifeline. It meant one thing for the prisoners in San Quentin, who perfectly understood the play when it was still generally found baffling, and another to audiences who had less grim reason to see life as a long waiting (for freedom, in that case). The act of waiting, we are left in no doubt, is the key action of the play. Godot could be simply the future, the unknown we are all bound to wait for.

Beckett brilliantly leaves the great question open for us to fill in according to our own imaginative needs; but God cannot be eliminated from the possible meanings, given Vladimir's preoccupation with the Crucifixion and the hope of salvation that is bound up with it. Two early pages of text [pp. 12–13] are given to establishing this preoccupation. Vladimir is shown to be both deeply involved with the Christ story and also realistically aware of the slenderness of the gospel evidence. Only 'one of the four says that one of the two was saved'. His doubts and his longing or fascination are equally strong; a position characteristic of modern thought it might be said. Many little verbal echoes hint at the link between his thinking about the Christian salvation and his concept of Godot. If Godot comes, he tells Estragon at the end [p. 94], they will be 'saved'. 'Saved from what?' Estragon had asked earlier, apropos the thief 'supposed to have been saved' [p. 12]. 'Hell' replies Vladimir, and then later, 'death'. This imagery of death and hell carries over into the real world of the action. 'I'm in hell!' Estragon cries (just before Pozzo's second entrance) taking refuge behind the tree, which turns out to be no use as a refuge [p. 74]. Perhaps the idea of being saved is an absurd one, as such episodes might suggest. Yet it is painfully real to the pair: their feelings about it take it into the realm of the tragic.

Whether Pozzo might be Godot is one of the horrific possibilities that also gets into the play, artfully linked with the idea of Godot as saviour and hence with the Bible stories. (The word 'crucify' is used [p. 34] of his treatment of Lucky. Though an 'Irishism', as Beryl and John Fletcher say,[5] the colloquialism cannot but retain some of its more serious meaning in this context.) Beckett abandoned an early idea of equating the two more closely but he left the characters still in considerable doubt. Even Vladimir is not sure if Pozzo is not Godot on his first appearance and Estragon twice mis-identifies him. 'I knew it was him' he says, when Pozzo and Lucky are strewn on the gound before

him [p. 77]. An aura of some other dimension hangs about
Pozzo: pagan mythology, perhaps or the God of the Old
Testament. 'I am perhaps not particularly human,' he says
in Act 1, 'but who cares?'. We might be tempted to
substitute 'less than human' but he thinks just the opposite,
using the biblical phrase 'in God's image' to mock at the
inferiority of Vladimir and Estragon: 'Of the same species
as Pozzo! Made in God's image!' [p. 23]. The verbal
construction brilliantly creates a troubling ambiguity. Is he
some monstrous God in whose image humanity was
created? There is enough cruelty in the play to sustain the
fearful question (a 'foul brood' is Vladimir's description of
his own species).

Ambiguity is preserved in the episodes which might have
been expected especially to undermine it, the arrival of
Godot's messenger. The Boy's two appearances towards the
end of each act bring hope and cancel it in the same breath.
He is the one young person in the play and the least
sophisticated, who speaks very simply and literally. Yet
from the start he introduces more mystery. He addresses
Vladimir inexplicably as Mr Albert and provokes a violent
reaction from Estragon [pp. 49–50] who accuses him of
telling a pack of lies. His words assure us that Godot exists,
and at the same time that he is not coming, at any rate, not
this evening. He seems to confirm the connection between
Godot and the God of the Bible by reporting on the work on
which he and his brother are engaged — looking after the
sheep and the goats, a familiar biblical metaphor. Then he
disconcertingly diverges from the familiar by revealing that
his brother who minds the sheep is beaten while he, who
minds the goats, is not.

Vladimir's line, 'Off we go again' (repeated in Act 2), tells
us that the Boy's message has been given before, every
evening we may assume. Vladimir's own return message,
'Tell him you saw us' followed by the question, 'You did see
us, didn't you?' becomes painfully intelligible in Act 2 when
the Boy does not recognise 'Mr Albert' and claims that this
is his 'first time'. In the variation on the question and
answer sequence that follows, we note that Vladimir's
questions no longer have a question mark attached to them

in the text. They have become statements he knows the Boy can do no more than confirm.

| | |
|---|---|
| VLADIMIR: | You have a message from Mr. Godot. |
| BOY: | Yes, sir. |
| VLADIMIR: | He won't come this evening. |
| BOY: | No, sir. |
| VLADIMIR: | But he'll come tomorrow. |
| BOY: | Yes, sir. |
| VLADIMIR: | Without fail. |
| BOY: | Yes, sir. |

[p. 91]

When he does ask a real question about the colour of Godot's beard, he gets a reply that depresses him: 'I think it's white, sir'. Beckett has suggested that this is because it makes Godot old; not a good omen for the future of the universe. It also seems to hint that the Boy is no nearer than Vladimir to knowing Godot; he too only 'thinks'. Estragon sleeps through the whole encounter: he is not so interested in the speculation (though emotional about the messenger). Vladimir's 'Christ have mercy on us!' brings them both closer to despair and into the suicide move, so absurdly and sublimely foiled by the discovery that the rope is only fit for holding up trousers. The text ends on the most telling of all its contradictions: the words say they will go, the stage direction says '*They do not move.*'

*Happy Days*

## 8 NOTE ON THE TEXT

The play was written in English and first published in 1961 (New York: Grove Press). It was first published in England in 1962 (Faber and Faber) and the 1966 edition of this is the text to which reference is made in this volume. Beckett's French translation, *Oh les beaux jours*, was published in Paris in 1963. An annotated edition containing both English and

French texts was published in 1978, edited by James
Knowlson. The text is contained in *The Complete Dramatic
Works* (Faber and Faber, 1986).

## 9   THE SITUATION

The situation is one of the strangest in the whole history of
theatre. In the first act a middle-aged woman, immured to
her waist in a mound of earth, addresses a more-or-less
continuous monologue to her husband whose head is just
visible above the slope at the back of her mound. Willie
seldom speaks. When he does, Winnie responds with joy:
'Oh you are going to talk to me today, this is going to be a
happy day!' [p. 19]. Other resources for seeing her through
her day are a capacious bag with a motley assortment of
possessions, including a musical-box and a revolver and a
parasol which catches fire when she puts it up. Her sleeping
and waking are controlled by a bell but she creates a time
world of her own, made up of memories, quotations, stories
and dreams, interspersed with rare dialogue. She sets the
musical-box playing the 'Merry Widow' waltz and Willie
joins in with the tune but she finds herself unable to sing. In
the second act Winnie has sunk further into the earth which
is now up to her neck: she cannot turn her head and can
indicate feeling only through her voice and her eyes and
facial movements. Willie is not heard or seen until the end
of the act but she continues to talk as if he were there,
reminding him of their romance, their wedding, the feelings
they once had. Finally Willie emerges from behind the
mound, an aged figure in wedding clothes, and crawls
toward her to be received with a mixture of delight and
other, more doubtful feelings. Now at last she is able to sing
'her' song, the 'Merry Widow' waltz. The play ends in a
long-held pause with Winnie looking down at Willie, still on
his hands and knees at the foot of the mound.

## 10   STRUCTURE AND SETTING

As the summary of the situation may indicate, it is scarcely possible to describe what happens in *Happy Days* without giving some account of small detail, since this is what makes up Winnie's constricted world. As in *Waiting for Godot*, the structure is highly symmetrical. Striking variations occur in the second act but they do not undermine the main effect of an action so meaningfully shaped that it cannot but repeat itself, up to a point. As in the earlier play, the action is seen to be running down in the second act which is briefer, more melancholy and dream-like. Both characters have a reduced physical presence in this act. Winnie cannot even move her head, Willie no longer offers even minimal conversation. We may find ourselves imagining a third act in which neither would be there at all. Yet it is in the second act, when the characters are so depleted, that a fantastic extension of life is achieved: Winnie's unquenchable flow of fancy is rewarded by the realisation of her dream of Act 1:

> What I dream sometimes, Willie. (*Pause.*) That you'll come round and live this side where I could see you. (*Pause. Back front.*) I'd be a different woman. (*Pause.*) Unrecognizable.
>
> [p. 35]

When Willie crawls towards her, it is the most spectacular of innumerable close links between the two acts. The structure artfully balances impressions of change and decay with those of continuity and continuance. In each act Winnie tells over her memories, prays, reflects on her situation, thinks about Willie, quotes half-remembered lines of verse, conjures up a vivid image of 'real' people (Mr and Mrs Shower or Cooker, who react unimaginatively to her plight) and declares her faith that the day 'will have been another happy day'. Each act opens with a piercing bell which causes her to open her eyes (summoning her imperiously towards the end of the second act, when she has apparently closed her eyes too soon).

The setting reinforces the symmetry of the dramatic

structure. Beckett's direction is for '*Maximum of simplicity and symmetry*', with Winnie in the '*exact centre*' of the mound. Originally this mound was to have been more geometrical, with shelves, a lower one supporting Willie. The more natural-looking mound in the text allows for freer-ranging associations: graves and ancient burial mounds at one extreme and erotic mounds (the mound of Venus) at the other. Both these extremes are contained within the flow of Winnie's thought, so it might be conjectured that the mound represents the way she sees life and herself. Such a view, however, requires a certain interpretation of Winnie's character: as we will see, there has been much critical disagreement on this point.

An important aspect of the set is the light, which Beckett describes in the text as '*blazing*'. The stage direction for Act 1 begins by describing '*expanse of scorched grass*' rising to the centre of the mound, a visual indication of the 'hellish heat' which Winnie complains of. There is no respite from this hot, bright light, presented in the text from time to time as a kind of hell or purgatory. Heat and fire are hinted at also in the colour of the scenic background, a '*very pompier trompe-l'oeil backcloth*'. (For French readers at least the phrase would have associations with fire, 'pompier' referring to the making of French fire engines.) The scene itself may strike a reader as either desolate or promisingly open, depending on temperament, perhaps: an unbroken plain and sky, presumably without clouds, recede to meet '*in far distance*'. What the scene and lighting designers make of these directions is an unknown which could affect nuances of interpretation. However, the set is dominated by the mound, which both raises Winnie above the earth and keeps her a prisoner of it.

## 11  RHYTHM, LANGUAGE AND STYLE

The rhythm of *Happy Days* is not altogether easy to feel for oneself from the text alone. It is made up in a remarkable

way from two separate rhythms, that of the speaking voice
and of small, apparently insignificant bodily movements.
Timing of absolute precision is demanded: this we can
indeed observe in the text, as in Winnie's opening prayer:

> (*gazing at zenith*). Another heavenly day. (*Pause. Head back level,
> eyes front, pause. She clasps hands to breast, closes eyes. Lips move in
> inaudible prayer, say ten seconds. Lips still. Hands remain clasped.
> Low.*) For Jesus Christ sake Amen. (*Eyes open, hands unclasp,
> return to mound. Pause. She clasps hands to breast again, closes eyes,
> lips move again in inaudible addendum, say five seconds. Low.*) World
> without end Amen.
>
> [pp. 9–10]

These instructions — '*say ten seconds*', '*say five seconds*', —
make it clear that the rhythm is being controlled as if it were
a piece of music Beckett were writing. Musical is a term
often rather loosely applied to melodious or highly rhythmic prose. Here it becomes relevant, even necessary. As
with music, it may not be easy to imagine the full effect
from the 'score' alone (the term seems to have some
appropriateness, if we are careful to remind ourselves, as
readers, that the notation refers to visual as well as verbal
timing). It is unlikely that there has ever been in the history
of theatre an opening monologue of such length and
musical exactness. Four pages of text [pp. 9–13] are given
to establishing Winnie's rhythm and style as a solo
performer. *Female solo*, we may recall, was how Beckett
thought of the play in the first place.

Winnie has to control her own rhythm in her long,
meandering, virtuoso monologues but she is also controlled
by a rhythm imposed from without, source unknown. The
bell that rings '*piercingly*' at the start of each act keeps the
same strict tempo, '*ten seconds*' and '*five seconds*'. Contrasting
with the shrill note of the bell which 'hurts like a knife' [p.
40] is the tinkle of the musical-box, heard late in Act 1 [p.
30] when Winnie unearths it from the jumble of her
belongings in the bag. This is a pretty, lilting sound yet it is
also, like the bell, mechanical, in the obvious sense that it is
made by a mechanical means. For readers, there may be

problems here. Those who have neither seen a production
nor heard the music have not much to go by: only the idea
of a musical-box and the rather banal words of the Merry
Widow waltz song (printed in the text) when Winnie finally
sings them at the end of the play. For a high climactic
moment, the words are hardly very inspiring:

> Though I say not
> What I may not
> Let you hear,
> Yet the swaying
> Dance is saying,
> Love me dear!

[p. 47]

Are we to take the musical-box episodes, we might ask, as
further evidence for something mechanical and undiscrimi-
nating in Winnie's tastes? The mechanical is certainly
stressed in recurring stage directions for her changes of
look. When she listens to the musical-box playing, her
'*happy expression*' appears, followed by an '*increase of happy
expression*' when Willie unexpectedly joins in with the tune,
singing wordlessly in a hoarse voice. Directions for Winnie's
smiles and expressions to go '*on*' and '*off*' are a curious
characteristic of the text which can sometimes be quite
comical, as in the direction '*Joy off*'.

Even without having production or waltz tune in mind, an
attentive reader will observe, however, that another, very
different emotional rhythm is drawn out by the musical-
box. The stage directions emphasise depth of feeling, in
Winnie's bodily movements, for instance. She first huddles
over the musical-box, then holds it to her breast with both
hands as she '*sways to the rhythm*'. The woman imprisoned in
earth is dancing to the lilting waltz tune, in memory
perhaps or in some corner of imagination. The verbal
rhythms also change, becoming more taut and poetic as she
accepts Willie's reluctance to give an encore and reflects on
the need for spontaneity in art. Gradually her style changes:
she moves away from her more clichéd and fulsome tones to

another level, where echoes of Shakespearean music are heard:

> . . . no, song must come from the heart, that is what I always say, pour out from the inmost, like a thrush. (*Pause.*) How often I have said, in evil hours, Sing now, Winnie, sing your song, there is nothing else for it, and did not. (*Pause.*) Could not. (*Pause.*) No, like the thrush, or the bird of dawning, with no thought of benefit, to oneself or anyone else.
>
> [p. 31]

If we pick up the echo from *Hamlet* in 'bird of dawning', it must carry with it a memory, however vague, of something magical and mysterious about bird song. The ghost of Hamlet's father faded on 'the crowing of the cock'. Marcellus notes the fact (Act I,i) and draws attention to the legend associated with that powerful dawn song. Mysteriously, it is heard all night long at the season 'Wherein our Saviour's birth is celebrated', dispelling apparitions and keeping the nights 'wholesome'. Winnie wants her song to have the selfless spontaneity of the bird's. Perhaps then, we may speculate, it would also acquire something of its miraculous power and dispel dubious or ominous apparitions. At the end of the act, when she tries for the song and fails, she immediately turns to prayer, so the Shakespearean link between natural and supernatural is in an odd way maintained:

> And now? (*Pause.*) Sing. (*Pause.*) Sing your song, Winnie. (*Pause.*) No? (*Pause.*) Then pray. (*Pause.*) Pray your prayer, Winnie.
>
> [p. 36]

The song is finally heard, words and all, when she sings it at the end of Act 2. It is at such a moment that the need for real sounds and sights becomes overwhelming. It is a hard task for the imagination to conjure up the image of the woman singing and estimate the effect of that song without the aid of concrete stage performance. For that reason, discussion of style in these fragile epiphanies is best left for the following section. That in itself is a measure of how crucial non-verbal effects are in this so-musical play.

The same remark applies to the intricate rhythmic structure of words, pauses, silences and sounds which Beckett has spun. It is true that we could hardly fail to observe this rhythm on the page, where every other sentence is often followed by a pause, and the stage directions slow down our reading of Winnie's words by continually telling us of each tiny movement she makes:

> (*She turns to bag, rummages in it, brings out finally a nailfile, turns back front and begins to file nails. Files for a time in silence, then the following punctuated by filing*) There floats up — into my thoughts — a Mr. Shower — a Mr. and perhaps a Mrs. Shower . . . .
>
> [p. 31]

We can certainly note the details, even the direction for silence, but it is not easy in reading to hold pauses and silent movements in mind or give them their proper weight. Readers generally want to speed on to words, not stop to register the rhythm of pauses and silent movements. In the theatre this becomes obligatory and Beckett takes advantage of the fact, as later discussion of the play in performance will show.

Easier for the reader to register is the rhythm of repetition which draws attention to key verbal phrases. However widely Winnie may ramble, she always returns to certain cherished sayings, tags, expressions of feeling: they are like rests where she pauses, draws mental breath, reminds herself of her own continuties. Chief among them is the 'happy days' motif, first heard early in Act 1, just after Willie becomes visible to the audience: 'Oh this is going to be another happy day!'. When Willie unexpectedly offers his opinion on a bilingual grammatical point [p. 19] she makes it clear how much her happy days depend in some way on him: 'Oh you are going to talk to me today, this is going to be a happy day!'. And so it continues throughout Act 1. The motif is triggered off by Willie's burst of hoarse song and by his long-delayed (but unusually full) reply to her request for a definition of hog. It is not heard at all in Act 2 so long as Willie remains silent, but returns at the very end after he has crawled over to her and managed to get out the one word, 'Win' [p. 47]. If we are attending to the fine detail in these psychological rhythms, we will have observed that the motif does not surface until Willie speaks. It is not enough for him to crawl; only when he croaks his *'just audible'* word does she produce her ritual response: 'Oh this *is* a happy day, this will have been another happy day!'.

Not all Winnie's key phrases are so intimately linked to Willie. Some are more generalised expressions of gratitude, for life, however it comes, we might say. 'That is what I find so wonderful' is one, and 'great mercies'. Occasional variations indicate her awareness of a need to modify her raptures, as when 'Wonderful' becomes 'comforting'. But 'wonderful' returns even in Act 2 [p. 42], where she is so much more deprived and on the whole the thankful phrases stay with her to the end. Repetition is in itself a comfort, so we may deduce from her use of phrases like 'I always find' and 'the old style'. The latter, one of the most habitual, is also the most mysterious. It is always used in relation to words denoting time: 'not a day goes by — (*smile*) — to speak in the old style — (*smile off*)' [p. 29]. Each time she uses the words and gives that smile she conveys her sense of being somehow out of time, in a region where the old vocabulary no longer applies though it is all she has got. It is for her the 'sweet old style' (an ironic variation on Dante's 'dolce stil nuovo').

Winnie's ability to refer to poets like Dante, and to quote from them, however incompletely, is a feature of her style that coexists (curiously, to some) with a taste for cliché and popular jingles. Her mind is full of all the things that have caught her fancy: she does not discriminate between high and low literature or other forms of culture, all are grist to her mill. Her language similarly expresses her all-embracing gusto. She can be racy and colloquial ('put a bit of jizz into it'), plain and simple, literary and witty, literary and affected ('tis only human', 'for naught'), recondite, bawdy. She is strongly histrionic and can do other people's style as well as her own mercurial one, the style of Mr Shower or Cooker, for instance, or Willie's in the days when he wooed her ('I worship you Winnie be mine'), rounding it off amusingly with words of her own, 'and then nothing from that day forth only titbits from *Reynolds' News*' [p. 46]. She is keenly interested in words, questioning Willie about anything he might be expected to know, like the definition of hog (from 'genuine hog's setae' on the toothbrush). She does not ask about setae, a word some might find obscure [p. 17]. Many of Winnie's quotations may seem to float into the mind unbidden: it is Beckett's art to fit them so naturally into all that is scatterbrained and random in her personality. But there is nothing random about their function: they have a very precise part to play in the pattern of thought which emerges, as it were, above Winnie's head. The lines from Shakespeare, Milton, Gray and the rest come chiming in, speaking of more than they seem to say, by virtue of their subtle placing in the fantastic situation. Winnie is by no means mistress of her quotations, a fact pointed up comically by her tendency to forget or slightly jumble them. Failing memory is partly to account for her lapses and the fact that, as Beckett says, she has 'a short span of concentration'. Often she is doing at least two things at once. Her first quotation (from *Hamlet*) comes when she is busily absorbed in cleaning her spectacles to get a better view of the writing on the toothbrush:

> — what are those wonderful lines — (*wipes one eye*) — woe woe is me — (*wipes the other*) — to see what I see —
> [p. 11]

When we fill in the missing words (not too difficult with this quotation from *Hamlet*) they bring with them above all a sense of shocking difference between things as they were and as they have become: 'O, woe is me T'have seen what I have seen, see what I see'.

What Winnie's erratic memory has dropped from the lines is that backward look of Ophelia's which stresses the tragic change made by time. Winnie takes plenty of backward looks herself, but she does not want to dwell on the tragic aspect. Stan Gontarski has shown that, in Beckett's radical revisions of early drafts, he worked precisely to this end, developing the comedy as 'a tonic, an elixir against the infection of pathos'.[6] Comic business frequently attends the quotations, as in Winnie's assiduous application of lipstick during her attempt to recall a passage from Milton:

> What is that wonderful line? (*Lips.*) Oh fleeting joys — (*lips*) — oh something lasting woe.
>
> [p. 13]

She is contemplating in her mirror the finished result of the lipsticking when she returns to Shakespeare for a quotation from another tragedy, *Romeo and Juliet*. What she gives us this time is even more fragmentary, to the point of being cryptic. 'Ensign crimson' she says, and then, laying down her lipstick and mirror (while Willie turns a page of his newspaper) 'Pale flag' [p. 14]. It is a fair bet that even quite well-read readers might fail to realise instantly (without aid of footnote) that 'Ensign crimson' is a shorthand allusion to Romeo's lines, 'beauty's ensign yet/Is crimson in thy lips and in thy cheeks'. After Winnie adds 'Pale flag', it might be easier to identify the source, though even then perhaps not to quote the whole line, in which Romeo wonders at the freshness of Juliet's beauty in the tomb: 'And death's pale flag is not advanced there'. Beckett plants these quotations in such a way that we have to work a little for them, like Winnie. One of their functions, it seems, is to inspire fellow-feeling. We could easily find ourselves, with Winnie, irritatedly asking ourselves, 'What is that unforgettable line?'

When the reader takes time to track the quotations to their sources and ponder their transformations, it soon becomes clear that no general statement about purpose could cover them all. Sometimes the quoting effect is, as noted, to increase the comedy. Or, more seriously, it may convey the sense of something incomplete about Winnie. Beckett described her to Billie Whitelaw when she was preparing the part as

> 'a mess. An organised mess . . . One of the clues of the play
> is interruption. Something begins, something else begins.
> She begins but she doesn't carry through with it. She's
> constantly being interrupted or interrupting herself. She's
> an interrupted being.'[7]

That certainly casts a graver light on the comedy of the
unfinished quotations. Often too the discrepancy between a
quotation and the situation of the speaker is a source of
irony, the *rire jaune* or sardonic laugh which Beckett has
attributed to Winnie. An example might be the cryptic
allusion in Act 2 to a passage in *Twelfth Night*:

> (*distends cheeks*) . . . even if I puff them out . . . (*eyes left, distends
> cheeks again*) . . . no . . . no damask.
>
> [p. 39]

Winnie's 'no damask' is a sad abbreviation. The extreme
verbal compression makes its own comment on the horrific
physical compression that is being imposed on her body.
Hands gone, hence mirror gone, the only way she can see
herself is by squinting down her nose at her puffed-out
cheeks. Not for her the expansiveness, or the romantic
melancholy of Viola's vision of beauty's erosion, the story of
the 'sister' who 'never told her love,/But let concealment
like a worm i' th' bud/Feed on her damask cheek'. It would
hardly be surprising if Winnie's memory of that image had a
caustic flavour; for her, unlike Viola, it is only too literally a
case of 'no damask'.

The quotation might also point to another motif in the
Shakespearean passage, the idea of 'concealment'. Winnie
doesn't seem to conceal much from Willie, it might be said.
Yet there are things she finds difficult to talk of, despite her
apparently uninhibited chattering. Quotation helps her in
her creative drive toward expressing and revealing all, as
when she remembers a favourite classic, 'I call to the eye of
the mind', the mesmeric opening line of Yeats's *At the
Hawk's Well*. This leads into a demonstration that even now,
in her near-coffin, Winnie can vividly bring characters to

life, as she invokes the Shower/Cooker couple, standing
there, as if in reality, gaping, asking 'Has she anything on
underneath?' [p. 43].

Winnie husbands her story-telling energies: the story of
Mildred is saved up for the time when Willie will fail her:
'There is always of course my story when all else fails' [p. 41].
Is this to be some kind of autobiography? There is a hint of
it in her preamble: 'A life. (*Smile.*) A long life. (*Smile off.*)'
Mildred 'will have memories, of the womb, before she dies',
a faintly ominous start to the tale. The story begins and
Winnie's vocabulary and tone take a conventional story-for-
children turn. Mildred scarcely emerges from behind the
dominating image of the 'big waxen dolly' which Winnie
describes, with pauses to get the detail right ('Pearly
necklace', 'A little picture-book'). Whether she is trying to
remember or invent, we cannot be sure: the story-teller gets
the upper hand, so Beckett suggests, with the direction,
'*Narrative*', which introduces an overtly literary line, 'The
sun was not well up . . .'. Something other than the literary
then intervenes. It is not one of her accidental self-
interruptions where she pulls herself up with 'Gently,
Winnie' at a dramatic point in the hitherto tame story:
'Suddenly a mouse —'. Nor is it any accident that she calls
for Willie: she needs his support here especially, and when
she fails to get it, reproaches him: 'I sometimes find your
attitude a little strange'.

'Strange' is one of Winnie's key words. Beckett stresses
this in Act 1 when she reflects on the oddity of having
recalled the Shower/Cooker couple:

> Strange thing, time like this, drift up into the mind. (*Pause.*)
> Strange? (*Pause.*) No, here all is strange.
>
> [p. 33]

On the next page she returns to the word, apropos her
thoughts on the mystery of the objects in her bag. She has
learnt that she was wrong in what she 'used to think', that
she could put them in and out 'indefinitely — back into the
bag — back out of the bag — until the bell — went'. The
wording throughout this sequence emphasises the struggle

she is having to reconcile the tenses: past, present and future:

> I suppose this — might seem strange — this — what shall I say — this what I have said — yes — (*she takes up revolver*) — strange (*she turns to put revolver in bag*) — were it not — (*about to put revolver in bag she arrests gesture and turns back front*) — were it not — (*she lays down revolver to her right, stops tidying, head up*) — that all seems strange. (*Pause.*) Most strange. (*Pause.*) Never any change. (*Pause.*) And more and more strange.
>
> [p. 34]

The passage shows several crucial features of her style, including the failure to finish, noted by Beckett. We might observe, however, that the outcome of her interrupting herself is that the much-discussed revolver, 'Brownie', remains on the mound, available in the last act (though, as it turns out, only to Willie). Hence, seeming indecisiveness might in this instance conceal a deep if unacknowledged intention.

Within this short space the word 'strange' is used four times. On the last occasion it draws attention to the dilemma at the heart of the play. Nothing changes: Winnie is trapped in a state of stasis and yet it does change, in that it becomes 'more and more strange'. The second act will show how true that is. 'Strange' is also an appropriate word for Winnie herself. She is no ordinary woman. Beckett said of her to Billie Whitelaw that she was 'a bit mad. Manic is not wrong but too big'. She certainly tells a strange story. Returning now, as Winnie does in Act 2, to the interrupted Mildred story, we may observe that she comes back to it after she has limbered up on the Shower/Cooker evocation [p. 43], almost as if she needed to exercise her story-telling muscles before she can face the more difficult task of finishing the tale of Mildred and the mouse which 'ran up her little thigh'. She interrupts herself at that point in a highly emotional way, with a piercing scream. It is meant to represent Mildred's reaction but we may wonder if it tells us of a trauma Winnie has herself endured, a rape or some other kind of shocking sexual experience. The dramatic effect of the episode is something best left for discussion in relation to performance, but it is worth noting here that Beckett cut from an early draft of the play passages endowing Winnie with a sexual appetite which might not have been consonant with the idea of traumatic pain.

Finally, we should consider for a moment the counter-pointing of Winnie's and Willie's styles. Willie has a coarser version of Winnie's relish for sayings and quotations. His first words are, in fact, a quotation from his favoured reading matter, the newspaper: 'His Grace and Most Reverend Father in God Dr. Carolus Hunter' has been found 'dead in tub' [p. 14], the last being Willie's gloss on a topic which for Winnie summons up romantic memories of Dr. Carolus ('Charlie Hunter' to her). Willie's next quotation has a different effect. His reading of an incongruous advertisement, 'Wanted bright boy', interrupts Winnie's reminiscences of yet another former beau at the very point when her gushing style — 'My first kiss!' — is shading into her genuinely poetic vein ('I see the piles of pots. (*Pause*) The tangles of bast. (*Pause*) The shadows deepening among the rafters' [p. 15]. The result is that she abandons the profounder vision and after a hurried revamp of her appearance, presumably for Willie's benefit, returns to the more mundane literary world of the toothbrush guarantee. Though infrequent, Willie's comments are thus a vital element in the close weaving of the text. He has no flights of fancy but he does once supply Winnie with a witty joke, when he explains the activity of the emmet that has appeared on the mound. 'Formication' he says and '*laughs quietly*' at his own near-pun, making Winnie laugh too [p. 24]. Her first inclination had been to call on God in a shudder of horror at the idea of life multiplying itself. Willie contri-butes more than meagre speech to the dialogue: his movements and showings of himself are equally important.

## 12 COMEDY OR TRAGEDY?

How this question is answered depends to some extent on the view taken of Winnie's character. Is she absurdly

unaware of her grim situation, forever trapped in a hellish
version of eternity, or is she aware and stoically enduring?
Opinion has been sharply divided on this point since the
play first appeared. It could of course be argued that
whatever we may think of Winnie, we are bound to be
appalled by her situation and pity her decline. Even if she is
seen as a clown, she becomes a tragic one in Act 2 when she
is being so mercilessly reduced. The tragic emotion,
however, is usually thought of as more complex than this
and the nature of the protagonist is part of the complexity.

Before pursuing that last point, we need to pause and
consider whether tragedy is a relevant term even to consider
applying to such a play. It would be easier (and, it could be
said, more appropriate) to settle for dark comedy or absurd
drama, forms which have been identified by modern
criticism as characteristic of our non-tragic times. It is true
that there is more absurdity in *Happy Days*, also that it has a
metaphysical resonance which goes far beyond the drama of
individual character. In this way the play approximates to
the idea of the absurd as notably defined by Martin Esslin.
Yet reactions to the play in performance suggest that the
word tragic keeps its place: something in the situation and
the character of Winnie call it out, along with words like
heroic or stoical which carry moral implications of the sort
that have always concerned tragedy.

Assuming that there is some point in discussing the
nature of the play in terms of comedy and tragedy (broadly
distinguished), we may return to the question of how
Winnie is to be seen, to what extent is she a tragic or a
comic figure. Much turns on the degree of awareness she
has. Beckett's own view, as expressed to Billie Whitelaw,
might seem to decide the matter and close the question.
'She's not stoic,' he said, 'she's unaware'. Questioning is
not closed by this remark, however; rather, in trying to
interpret it, we move ever deeper into the play. In the first
place, we can identify certain kinds of awareness that
Winnie clearly has. She is not such an 'incurable optimist'
(so she was disdainfully described by an early reviewer) that
she can fail to observe the inexorable inroads made by time
on her charms and faculties. At the very start of the play she

is observing her own decay, examining the state of her teeth and exclaiming 'Good God!'. Admittedly, she follows this up with one of her 'silver lining' reassurances:

— no better — no worse — (*lays down mirror*) — no change — (*wipes fingers on grass*) — no pain — (*looks for toothbrush*) — hardly any — (*takes up toothbrush*) — great thing that —
[p. 18]

But we might ask, what else could she do? Then again, it might be said that she goes ridiculously too far in her expressions of gratitude to providence (or God or whatever she has in mind when she talks of 'great mercies'). Could there be anything more absurdly incongruous, coming from someone immured in earth up to her waist, than that happy opening line, 'Another heavenly day'? Beckett deliberately stressed the religious allusion (and the irony of it) by changing the 'glorious' of an early draft to the more significant 'heavenly'. Winnie is not altogether unaware of that irony. She has second thoughts about describing the bright light that is trained relentlessly on her as 'holy light'. One of her most truncated and throwaway quotations (suggestive in this instance of deep familiarity with the source) is from Milton's moving invocation at the opening of Book III of *Paradise Lost*: 'Hail, holy light'. She has hardly come out with the words before she is changing them to express an opposite view of this oppressively steady light. (She is polishing her spectacles as she talks, in the effort to read the difficult writing on the toothbrush):

(*polishes*) — holy light — (*polishes*) — bob up out of dark — (*polishes*) — blaze of hellish light.
[p. 11]

Do we laugh here as perhaps we did earlier, at 'Another heavenly day'? And do we laugh at the opening of Act 2 when she gives us the full Miltonic phrase, 'Hail, holy light', from her terrible new position, imprisoned up to her neck? These questions are best left for fuller discussion from an audience viewpoint, in the next section. The reader may

find it harder to estimate the effect of the delicate changes
made by the stage situation on words that do not themselves change. On the other hand, in reading there is more
time to ponder the ramifications of the literary allusions.
We might recall that Milton's invocation of 'holy light' was
written when he was in a situation as bitter as Winnie's. She
might even have it in mind when she says near the
beginning of Act 1, straining to read the toothbrush legend,
'blind next'. Milton's continuing to invoke 'holy' light is not
taken as a sign that he was unaware of the darkness in
creation. It is harder to be sure what Winnie perceives but it
would have to be said that she sees clearly enough her own
decline and her vulnerability to disaster. The worst would
be the loss of Willie, and she is allowing herself to imagine
this at the very start of the play, long before he falls silent:

> Whereas if you were to die — (*smile*) — to speak in the old
> style — (*smile off*) — or go away and leave me, then what
> would I do, what *could* I do, all day long . . .
>
> [p. 18]

In what way, then, is Winnie unaware? At this point we need
to take into account the many levels and layers of meaning
which can be traced in the play, meanings Winnie herself
may not perceive, or not understand fully. What is the
meaning of the place she is in? This crucial question has
been answered along many different lines: theological,
philosophical, sociological . . . . Hints have been found in
Beckett's essay on Joyce where he notes philosophical
concepts such as Vico's 'preordained cyclism of history'.
This has a possible relation to the perpetual recurrences in
*Happy Days*. The parasol will always be back for next
performance, and will burn again every night because it
once did so. Winnie, in fact, draws attention to this bit of
Vico in her sly little metatheatrical joke: 'I presume this has
occurred before, though I cannot recall it' [p. 28]. Other
reflections in the Joyce essay may throw light on the bizarre
stasis in which Winnie is trapped, as for instance, the idea
that 'The maxima and minima of particular contraries are
one and indifferent' or that hell and paradise are, equally,

conditions of 'static lifelessness'.[8] (Only purgatory, the state between, can offer change and therefore life though also, inevitably, decay and death.) From this point of view, Winnie's prayer, 'World without end' takes on a dark quality. A bleak vision is evoked (for us if not for her) of grim alternatives: change, which means decay, and a stasis, whether of hell or heaven, which means endless repetition or recycling.

The idea of nothing coming to an end, of a suffering consciousness continuing for ever, familiar in traditional religious concepts of hell, was most famously given literary expression by one of Beckett's admired authors, Dante. Whiffs of the hell in *The Divine Comedy* have been detected in *Happy Days*. In the play too, physical torment, including the classic heat of hell-fire, is accompanied by the mental pain of forever retelling a life story. There is one obvious difference in that Dante's sufferers were being punished for their sins. Winnie is hardly to be considered a great sinner. Critics have seen her more often as an everywoman (a tag that would, however, be treated witheringly by feminist criticism). Her sin, if that is what it is, consists in having been born. Hers is simply the natural lot, seen from a modern perspective, probably agnostic, in which there is no clearly divine aspect to the concept of eternity: the 'static lifelessness' of hell and heaven cannot be distinguished, one from one another. Perhaps it is the awesome bleakness of this perspective which Winnie has not fully grasped. If she had, she might cease to say her prayers or cherish quotations which speak of heavenly dimensions.

She does, of course, have glimmerings of the terrible possibility that there might be no significance in her sufferings. In Act 2 she wonders whether it is not 'Just chance' that the hellish heat is not 'the eternal cold. (*Pause.*) Everlasting perishing cold' [p. 39]. But she is able to push the dark thought away with the determinedly optimistic addition, 'happy chance. (*Pause*) Oh yes, great mercies, great mercies'. Similarly, she is troubled by momentary intuitions that time is a wrecker, not just of her physical state (she always sees that clearly) but of her whole being, her identity. Is the Winnie who is remembering Charlie

Hunter and, more tentatively, Mr Johnson ('or Johnston' or
perhaps I should say John*stone*' [p. 15]) the same Winnie
who acquired the memory in her youth? We are in Proustian
territory here and might recall that when Beckett wrote on
Proust he described Time as an element in a 'monster or
Divinity', bound up with Habit and Memory. Speaking of
Proust's 'creatures', he announced that there was no escape
from the hours and days, from yesterday, because 'yesterday has deformed us, or been deformed by us . . . . We are
not merely more weary because of yesterday, we are other,
no longer what we were before the calamity of yesterday'.[9]

Winnie thus demonstrates human confusion in the face of
universal dilemma. Like most people, she wants somehow
to hold on to past time without being stuck in it; hence the
endless rehearsal of her memories. Her critics have pointed
out that she also seems to be trapped in a condition
described by another of Beckett's esteemed authors, Scho-
penhauer, who wrote of the difficulty of 'being' anywhere
but in the present: 'The form of the phenomenon of will, the
form of life or reality, is really only the present, not the
future or the past'. Winnie fumbles with this problem in her
hesitations over tenses and intermittently reveals a deep
anxiety over it:

> Then . . . now . . . what difficulties here, for the mind. (*Pause.*)
> To have been always what I am — and so changed from what
> I was. (*Pause.*) I am the one, I say the one, then the other.
> (*Pause.*) Now the one, then the other.
>
> [p. 38]

But these concepts are too heavy for her to support. She
escapes, as so often, into her habit of not finishing, of
interrupting her own train of thought. She has in full
measure what Beckett once called 'our smug will to live' and
though she can picture her own end — 'Shall I myself not
melt perhaps in the end . . . little by little be charred to a
black cinder' — she will not give up the habitual reactions,
the prayers, the expressions of thankfulness which help to
keep her going, even though she may also wish she could
end.

How does her attitude to Willie fit into this double-levelled awareness which Beckett maintains throughout the text? On one level her need for him requires no special interpretation: it is the usual need of someone long married for the partner, however unsatisfactory in some way he may be. From a more philosophical viewpoint, it can be seen as the need for reassurance about her very existence. Her sense of her own identity depends on Willie being there to acknowledge it. 'Esse est percipi', the epigraph Beckett attached to *Film*, has a more desperate side to it in an age which doubts the existence of God. Its perpetrator, Bishop Berkeley, whose idealist philosophy plays a part in Beckett's thinking, held that only by being perceived can anything be said to exist, but as God existed, He perceived all and kept all in existence. Winnie may not be familiar with Berkeleyan thought, but she appears to have an uneasy intuition of it when she makes her assertion in Act 2, without sight or sound of Willie, that 'Someone is looking at me still' [p. 37] and 'proves' Willie's continuing existence from the fact that she is still talking. She could not continue to talk without an audience 'in the wilderness': 'Ergo you are there'.

The Winnie of Act 2 seems to have been forced into increased awareness, 'deep trouble for the mind' [p. 38]. Everything has been reduced and she can no longer enjoy so well as she did in Act 1 her spasmodic philosophisings: ('I hope you caught something of that, Willie, I should be sorry to think you had caught nothing of all that, it is not every day I rise to such heights' [p. 30]). In Act 2, we observe, *such aperçus* tend to lead into silences, as in the sequence where she brings the sunshade into play, though now only as a form of words, for it has disappeared from the scene:

The sunshade you gave me . . . that day . . . (*Pause*) . . . that day . . . the lake . . . the reeds. (*Eyes front. Pause.*) What day? (*Pause.*) What reeds? (*Long pause. Eyes close. Bell rings loudly. Eyes open. Pause. Eyes right.*) Brownie of course. (*Pause.*) You remember Brownie, Willie, I can see him. (*Pause.*) Brownie is there, Willie, beside me. (*Pause. Loud.*) Brownie is there, Willie. (*Pause. Eyes front.*) That is all.

[pp. 39–40]

How we are to interpret the strange reminder about
Brownie is one of the ambiguities we might hope for
performance to illuminate. In fact, as we will see, Beckett
maintained most carefully in production the equivocal
nature of the Brownie episode. The text too leaves open the
questions, how are we to react to Winnie and is hers a tragic
situation? As the foregoing discussion may have suggested,
our answers must to some extent depend on our reading of
what the situation means. As that is to do with the meaning
of life, it would be surprising if we could all agree on it but
one thing we surely must agree, that Winnie's character is
complex, enough so to make a tragic reading at least
possible.

# PART TWO: PERFORMANCE

## 13 GENERAL NOTE

A very special situation exists where the relation of Beckett's texts to performance is concerned. Beckett began directing his own plays in the sixties, setting dauntingly high standards of precision and control. The Production Notebooks he kept on these occasions provide a wonderfully illuminating record not only of his directorial decisions but also of his changing thoughts on the plays. In the interval (often long) between writing a work and directing it, his view of the play had sometimes changed quite radically. *Waiting for Godot*, for instance, seemed to him 'Messy' and 'not well thought out' when he returned to it as director, with by then considerable stage experience. It has followed that in directing his plays he has tended to rewrite them in a minor way, making small but significant cuts, changing a line or a visual arrangement and so forth. These were production changes and might have been thought of as not affecting the text. But because they have proceeded from so authoritative a source they have already, in advance of new texts appearing, acquired a strange, shadowy, textual life. Directors who know of Beckett's amendments have sometimes (as we will see) incorporated them into their own productions, using the 'other' text which is seen as superseding the printed one.

Beckett has facilitated this process by making his Production Notebooks available in the Samuel Beckett Archive in the University of Reading. They are also being published, under the general editorship of Professor James Knowlson. The first has already appeared (Faber and Faber, 1985) and is the Production Notebook for *Happy Days*, edited by James Knowlson. It will be followed by the *Waiting for Godot* Notebook, edited by Dougald McMillan and James Knowlson.

It is a measure of the general respect for Beckett's skills as a
director (as well as author) that directors have not waited
for new texts to be published but have responded to the
sense of 'work in progress' that has emanated from
Beckett's theatrical activity. The Production Notebooks,
suggests James Knowlson, 'reveal what clearly represents a
further phase in the writer-director's creative effort, as he
re-experiences his own play and envisages it concretely in
theatre space' (*Happy Days Production Notebook*, p. 13).
Observant readers of the text who were puzzled by
variations in the 1987 production of *Waiting for Godot* at the
National Theatre were therefore witnesses of a rather
unusual phenomenon.

Beckett's own records have been valuably reinforced by
accounts of the rehearsal process made by members of his
production teams and by scholars such as Ruby Cohn,
James Knowlson, Stanley Gontarski, and Dougald McMillan
and Martha Fehsenfeld the last two in their book *Beckett in
the Theatre*. They have provided invaluable guides to the
fascinating detail of Beckett's thinking on the theatrical
effects he needs and on his view of his plays. (A few crucial
works are listed at the end of this volume.) Beckett's
productions have powerfully affected those of us who have
had the good fortune to see any of them. They cannot but be
thought of as in a class of their own: it would hardly be
possible to discuss the text in performance without some
reference to them. Indeed, reverberations from them have
already been felt (necessarily) in the preceding discussion
on texts. However, as the very special German productions
have already received such close study and been so fully
charted, I propose to give no more than a brief summary of
their general effect and otherwise draw on them simply as
occasion demands.

## 14   CHOICE OF PRODUCTIONS

Beckett's plays have attracted so many fine and interesting
stage presentations that in selecting only two for each of our

plays, many must be omitted that would obviously have figured in a fuller account. To give a stage history is not the purpose of this volume. If it were, the first productions of both plays, in English and French, would obviously have had to be included. So far as *Waiting for Godot* is concerned, these were adventures into a most strange unknown, especially the first of all, Roger Blin's *En attendant Godot* at the Théâtre de Babylone (15 January 1953), but also Alan Schneider's stressful American production with Bert Lahr as Estragon at the Coconut Grove, Miami (3 January 1956) and Peter Hall's, the first British production, at the Arts Theatre Club, London (3 August 1955). As there is much easily accessible commentary available on these early productions (especially now that Blin's has been examined in fascinating detail by Ruby Cohn, see Note 2) it seems reasonable to make reference to them only when the discussion demands it. So also with the first performances of *Happy Days*. By the time it appeared, Beckett's theatre had become a little more familiar to more people and the focus in accounts of the first productions comes to rest more on the actress playing Winnie than on the director. This time the first-ever was by an American actress, Ruth White, at the Cherry Lane Theatre, New York (17 September 1961), followed by Brenda Bruce in the first British production, at the Royal Court Theatre (1 November 1962). Beckett's French version, *Oh les beaux jours* at the Odéon, Paris (21 October 1963) established itself as one of the longest running (or recurring) productions of any of his plays, with an exquisitely tailored performance by Madeleine Renaud and by Jean-Louis Barrault as a humorously recalcitrant Willie.

Though I do not intend to focus on them specifically, there must be occasional reference to these first productions, which had the special virtue (whatever their mistakes) of uncovering totally new forms of dramatic art. They sometimes drew revealing comments and advice from Beckett. Peter Hall records[10] that when Beckett came to see the rehearsals of his 1955 production, he commented that it was fine 'but you don't bore the audience enough. Make them wait longer. Make the pauses longer. You should bore them'. This advice was, and remains, an important clue to the way Beckett conceives the rhythm of a production and the purpose of that rhythm. The audience have to be drawn into the position of the characters, and for Vladimir and Estragon that means, above all, waiting: 'Make them wait longer'.

To recapitulate and outline the arrangement to follow. Apart from occasional illustration from productions of note (and reference to the Schiller-Theater productions of each play) I will focus on four British productions, including one directed by Beckett. The earliest of the four is the 1975 production of *Happy Days* with Peggy Ashcroft as Winnie, the latest the 1987 production of *Waiting for Godot*, both at the National Theatre, London.


*Waiting for Godot*

### 15   NOTE ON THE SCHILLER-THEATER WEST BERLIN 1975 PRODUCTION


In his production of *Waiting for Godot* at the Schiller-Theater, West Berlin, Beckett revealed the play as a thing of haunting beauty, droll and deeply sad at once, a tragicomedy, exactly as he describes it in the text. Those who saw it in Berlin or, as I myself did in London when it came to the Royal Court Theatre the next year, would surely feel that Peter Hall (who knew from experience the difficulties) had found the right words when he praised the 'Absolute precision, clarity, hardness. No sentimentality, no indulgence, no pretension'.[11] Bareness and purity are other words that come to mind, yet along with these austere qualities went a sense of fun and tenderness, liable to break out at any minute like a sudden, unexpected smile.

The '*country road*' of the rendezvous was simply the bare stage, its essential nature defined by the tree, a minimal, slender, dun-coloured stem, branching into three, and one other object, similarly coloured, a stone (rather than the

'*low mound*' specified in the text). This stone, the only resting
place, was used chiefly by Estragon, whose proneness to
dropping off to sleep afforded some of the production's
most delicate moments of feeling. When he woke with a
start in Act 1, for instance, complaining, 'Why will you
never let me sleep?', the expression on the actor's face,
confusion spreading into shocked disappointment, perfectly
rendered the suggestion in the text that Estragon's dreams
are not always nightmares. Dreaming is also a release or a
delight; in waking he is 'restored to the horror of his
situation'.

Whatever they were doing, the appearance of the two
always carried associations with the comic pairs dear to
Beckett and familiar to us all from Laurel and Hardy or
Marx Brothers films. (For anyone seeing this production,
with its wonderfully straight-faced fooling, it would be no
surprise to learn that the juggling game with the bowler
hats in Act 2 derived from *Duck Soup*.) Stefan Wigger's very
tall, lean Vladimir looked down on the dumpy Estragon of
Horst Bollmann, a balancing act interestingly compared by
Ruby Cohn with the scenic pattern: 'squat stone almost
imitating Estragon and tall tree Vladimir'.[12] Perhaps this
more poetic matching contributed to the extraordinarily
touching quality of the scene at the end when the two were
left standing in a cold white light, jokes over, with nothing
to keep them company but each other, the stone and the
tree — and the far-distant moon. It was one of those rare
theatrical images which one feels sure will remain in the
memory forever.

Little things like the boots that give Estragon so much
trouble had an unrestrained double life in this production.
They were at once perfectly ordinary — Horst Bollmann's
great gift for human naturalness (even in the thick of a
comic turn) left no doubt that those boots really hurt — yet
by the end they had become something like a symbol of
what it was to be human. When he sat down on the stone for
the last time to wrestle with the ill-fitting objects, groaning
(in German) 'My feet!' and then, 'Help me!', it was a cry
from the heart that (without seeming to try) lifted the
prosaic misery of bad feet into the empyrean. The sadness

was almost more than one could bear when Vladimir turned away to ask himself, very quietly and searchingly, 'Was I sleeping while the others suffered? Am I sleeping now?'. There was no need for great command of German to recognise from Stefan Wigger's finely judged changes of tone the transition from that deeply human moment to the more mystical vein induced by the poignant sight of the sleeping Estragon: 'At me too someone is looking, of me too someone is saying, he is sleeping, he knows nothing, let him sleep on'.

Other moments stand out in memory with great force. Never can the act of language have seemed such a fantastic event as when Lucky, played with hypnotic concentration by Klaus Herm, broke his long silence to exude, without expression, the appalling flow of the think. The mysterious bond between him and his master, the jovially assertive Pozzo presented by Carl Raddatz, was subtly established by their silent communications over such things as the bones, what Beckett in his Notebook called their 'hypno look'. Beckett evidently selected his cast for this production with the idea of symmetrical visual oppositions (tall, short; thin, plump) to the fore. But he also stressed interchangeability, as in the switching around of costume which had Vladimir and Estragon reverse the order of their complementary coats and trousers from one act to the next.

Perhaps the most difficult of the episodes, those with the Boy, showed most clearly the value to the production of Beckett's controlling hand. It had the simplicity of a dream but a dream that for its duration seemed more real than everything around it. There was a delicate, slow graduation, from the painful resignation of the questions that are no questions, through Vladimir's outburst of angry frustration to the drained quiet of the final sequence, when the moon came up and after the suicide that is no suicide, everything became totally still. It was clear that they were, as Beckett has said, exhausted: there was no more to be done.

These poetic or tender moments worked without falling into the 'tear trap' Roger Blin saw as a potential hazard to him as a director. Beckett had made sentimentality impossible by his strong comic emphasis, often close to the impersonality of farce or music-hall routine, and by a general austerity of speech and movement. The changes he introduced often heightened the stylisation: like the characters in *The Importance of Being Earnest* Vladimir and Estragon spoke in chorus the question about getting rid of Lucky which is asked by Vladimir alone in the text, 'You waagerrim?' [p. 32]. The cuts he made were usually to do with strengthening the austerity, tightening or clarifying the text. Pozzo lost some comic busines and some words, often understandably, as with the technically awkward crack of the whip [p. 37], or the obscure word, 'knook' [p. 33] (which Beckett invented, by analogy with 'knout' and has now dropped). Sometimes the cuts were more disconcerting, for instance, the removal of Pozzo's sinister line, 'He refused once'. It is around Pozzo, in fact, that the most controversial changes have been made, in both this and the 1984 production, which Beckett directed (up to a point, in limited time) with Rick Cluchey's San Quentin Company. I will refer to this much-debated production when discussing the second of the two British productions I have chosen to focus on. Now, however, we turn to the first.

16  ROYAL EXCHANGE THEATRE COMPANY, MANCHESTER, 1980

Max Wall as Vladimir, Trevor Peacock as Estragon, Wolfe Morris as Pozzo, Gary Waldhorn as Lucky, Jacob Murray/ Clive Myers as A Boy. Directed by Braham Murray. Opened 13 November 1980.

In electing to illustrate from this, rather than, say, the much acclaimed 1964 production with Nicol Williamson as Vladimir and Jack MacGowran as Lucky (staggering performances both), I have had in mind the close attention which, as I mentioned earlier, has already been paid to works in which Beckett has had a hand. (He worked on that production with Anthony Page, the director, and gave close advice to Jack MacGowran, his friend as well as admired actor.) Turning now to productions in which Beckett was not directly involved, that at the Royal Exchange Theatre suggested itself for two particular reasons. One is to do with the nature of the theatre building where the play was performed, the other with the casting of Max Wall as Vladimir.

The overwhelming impression made by the Royal Exchange Theatre is of enclosure within towering empty space. Carved out of the original Royal Exchange building, it was envisaged from the start as a theatre that would not attempt to disguise its untheatrical origins but make positive use of them. It is a flexible space (no fixed proscenium) and there is an exhilarating sense of free relationship with the undefined surrounding areas of the inherited structure. For the 1980 production of *Godot*, the blocks in which the audience were dispersed (on the same level as the actors) were crossed by trackways through which the performers entered the acting space. To be seated at the end of a row was to feel quite perilously close to Pozzo and Lucky as they made their strange exits and entrances, close enough to touch as they passed.

The detail of the smallest physical movement was highlighted by this scenic arrangement which made one aware in an immediate, physical way of effects not instantly apparent from the text (particularly to anyone who had not previously seen a production). It was sharply noticeable, for instance, that the Pozzo/Lucky pair follow their own line and are never diverted from it, despite all distractions and hesitations. Our proximity to the performers made it easier to share in Vladimir's surprise when Pozzo prepared to continue his journey to the fair in the same direction from which he and Lucky had entered. His comment, 'You're going the wrong way' [p. 47] expressed our own immediate thought, and prompted further thought, on another level, about the nature of 'the way'. It was also easy, rather alarmingly, to imagine Pozzo paying out his rope to the full to get his 'running start' somewhere in the dark fringe around us. We were uneasily close to everything; the crack of the whip and the grotesquely resounding roars that preceded the Pozzo/Lucky entrance, the shout of 'Stand back!' that announced Pozzo's return from the wrong exit.

Lucky in the meantime was stranded among us, an uneasy situation for everybody. There he stood, mute, expressionless, rope hanging slack round his neck, close to us physically yet utterly apart. He was in a world of his own where only he and Pozzo existed. What came through above all was his need to wait there. He was waiting for Pozzo as the other two were waiting for Godot. It was one of the many moments when the distinctive stage space helped to illuminate subtle thematic suggestions; in this case, the suggestion discussed earlier that there are mysterious connections between the unlike pairs, even that they can be seen as aspects of one psyche. There was a sense of relief when the waiting came to an end and Lucky began to move across the space in the right direction, having received the command 'On!' from Pozzo, still out of sight on the wrong side taking his running start. There had been a curious sense of discomfort at being left alone with this pallid, hopeless looking creature. It was disturbing to be close to someone who almost ceased to be without his tyrant to command him. Least of all could we expect him to entertain us. Lucky on his own was a kind of nothing, capable only of still inspiring alarm. Curiously, we wanted the tyrant back. Pozzo seemed in his ominous way at home in the space as he swaggered across it, rope and whip in hand, the archetypal ringmaster, instigator of roars and provider of entertainment.

Circus comparisons would have been hard to avoid with this production, given the natural kind of ring made by the audience and the physical proximity to the performers, all reinforcing the ringmaster suggestion in the Pozzo role. Roger Blin had considered the circus analogy one of the traps he would beware of, rightly, for to overdo any one line of interpretation would be false to the play. It was written so as to evade definition and functions on many levels. On one of these, however, the circus analogy has force. The hint of it in Braham Murray's production helped to bring out the idea of circularity, which in other ways too his handling of the stage space highlighted, making it physically very vivid.

For the Royal Exchange audience it was immediately obvious when Pozzo came back to the space from his running start, playing out the tautened rope, that it was he who was following Lucky, not the other way round. Thus when they reappeared at their original point of entry through the audience in Act 2, Lucky still ahead, they created an immediate impression of having completed a circling movement round us. Everything was going round and round, the whole circus. A wonderfully dream-like, rather chilling effect, reinforced aurally by the repetitive sound of Lucky dropping the baggage (off-stage on leaving in Act 1, on-stage when returning in Act 2). In the distinctive Royal Exchange space, this purely physical, wordless movement worked as a natural symbol, pointing us to other, more abstract circlings, the 'preordained cyclism' Beckett spoke of in his Joyce essay, perhaps. When Pozzo gave his terse answer, 'Sand' to Vladimir's question 'What is there in the bag?', he was talking, though so cryptically, in a way we could understand. Thoughts about the 'sands of time' and the cyclical nature of history sprang naturally to mind in this context.

The special shape of the theatre also helped to establish an immediate and very personal sense of fellow feeling with Vladimir and Estragon. We were not sitting in the stalls at a safe distance but along with them in a large empty space with a sandy floor, feeling exposed and also enclosed (the many doors heard shutting from time to time were a reminder of enclosure as well as of the further stretches of undefined space beyond.) This was a very direct simulacrum of the characters' situation. In so open a theatre with so few fixed points, talk of the void seemed entirely natural. We too were in some compartment of it, our only landmark the tree — and the actors, who defined the space for us simply by being there. It seemed natural too that they should be aware of us and make their mischievous, oblique allusions to the fact. Trevor Peacock came right up to a front row, jovially offering his embrace as he declared, 'Charming spot' and 'Inspiring prospects' [pp. 14–15]. The audience were thoroughly implicated in the questions: why are we here, are we in the right place?

Representing one production only, these pictures are all taken from *Waiting for Godot* at the Royal Exchange Theatre, Manchester, 13 November–20 December 1980.

1. The Royal Exchange Theatre, Manchester. Photograph © Kevin Cummins.

2. Max Wall (*right*) as Vladimir and Trevor Peacock as Estragon. Photograph © Kevin Cummins.

3. Wolfe Morris (*right*) as Pozzo and Gary Waldhorn as Lucky. Photograph © Kevin Cummins.

4. Max Wall (*right*) as Vladimir and Trevor Peacock as Estragon. Photograph © Kevin Cummins.

5. Wolfe Morris (*left*) as Pozzo and Gary Waldhorn as Lucky. Photograph © Kevin Cummins.

6. Max Wall as Vladimir. Photograph © Kevin Cummins.

ESTRAGON:     In my opinion we were here.
VLADIMIR:     (*looking round*) You recognise the place?
ESTRAGON:     I didn't say that.
VLADIMIR:     Well?
ESTRAGON:     That makes no difference.
VLADIMIR:     All the same . . . that tree . . . (*turning towards the auditorium*) . . . that bog.

[p. 15]

The textual direction makes it clear that Beckett wanted the audience drawn in at such points. Larry Held, who played Estragon for Rick Cluchey, spoke out to the audience (under Beckett's direction) at other points, not so marked in the text; 'Where are all these corpses from ?' [p. 64] and 'There's no lack of void' [p. 66]. His Vladimir, Bud Thorpe, told Colin Duckworth, presumably as a result of the rehearsal experience, that he thought Beckett 'does purposely want to smash that fourth wall'. The Royal Exchange Theatre allowed this wish to be realised in a way that was natural and also unnerving, since mostly the actors took no direct notice of us and were completely taken up with their games. We were being drawn into them when they spoke to us, and anything could happen, a rather dangerous sensation (especially for those who knew Max Wall's ability to have somewhat demonic fun with his music-hall audiences).

Perhaps the most impressive of all the effects the theatre shape made possible were those to do with the Boy. His voice calling 'Mister' [p. 49] in Act 1 came from another point in that same empty space into which Pozzo and Lucky had just disappeared somewhere around us. It was 'our' space but one that was concealed and unknown to us: a very fine, poetic effect, this. Perhaps because he could be heard coming from far off, he seemed to trail with him some natural mystery from his distant provenance. This gave tremendous force and poignancy to the simple answers in the questioning sequence. His initial nervousness was entirely credible in relation to the raucous sounds made by Pozzo, the whip and the roars. His shrinking from the noisy show in which Vladimir and Estragon had found entertainment emphasised his absolute distance from them. Some perception of that sort seemed to explain Estragon's violent reaction when the Boy claimed to be 'a native of these parts', a violence which fed into his sorrowful acceptance of the gulf between, 'I'd forgotten'. The great physical impact of the Boy's entry made it much easier for the young actors alternating in the role to convey without strain the sense of someone remote, whose words are a mystery, yet who is also just a boy, simply speaking what he knows about matters familiar to him. We could both believe and be astounded and disbelieving as he came out with his account of life with Godot in terms of the Bible stories: the sheep and the goats, the two of whom one was saved (that is, not beaten) and the other damned. For him, clearly, it was no more than a straightforward account of the treatment meted out by Godot to his brother and to him. Why one was beaten he did not know; whether he himself was unhappy he did not know. When Vladimir commented, on that last, 'You're as bad as myself', the aged actor and the young boy became close in a moment of extreme poignancy, before they diverged, as we knew they had to. The Boy returned to the dark space around us, really running, as the text requires and the flat, ample space allowed, until he disappeared into an unseen which seemed all the more distant for the running feet. These were thrilling moments indeed, opening up an almost unimaginable dimension in which the Boy was running all the way to Godot, that being we were never going to see for ourselves.

Braham Murray drew such strong and haunting effects from this distinctive theatre space as to make it seem the play's natural and ideal context: one began to wonder how the proscenium stage could compete. The emphasis was on space rather than setting. Something was lost by the absence of the moon prescribed in the text. The spectral blue light that flooded the scene for the change to moonlight could not create the curious blend of artifice and poetry in the text's account of the moon appearing so suddenly, as it rises, mounts the sky and '*stands still, shedding a pale light on the scene*'. But still, the theatre space, bathed in that atmospheric light, exerted to the end its power to suggest itself as the void from which the actors have no exit.

I turn now to the second major reason for choosing to

illustrate from this production, the fact that Vladimir was played by Max Wall, a veteran music-hall comedian. This was something unusual in the British stage history of the play, though by no means unprecedented. Roger Blin, a great fan of silent film comics — Keaton, Chaplin, Harry Langdon — cast a music-hall artist, Lucien Raimbourg, as the very first Vladimir and Alan Schneider introduced Estragon to America (at the unlikely venue of the Coconut Grove Playhouse, Miami) in the person of a celebrated comic, Bert Lahr (the Cowardly Lion of *The Wizard of Oz*). The latter piece of casting provided a curious, if at the time trying demonstration of how well Beckett has captured the flavour of music-hall in the more subtle versions perfected by Vladimir and Estragon. Schneider described ruefully how Lahr soon recognised the likeness to vaudeville routines of the pair's 'ping-pong games' and began to insist on his right, as the 'top banana' to have all the best laugh lines to himself: Vladimir was only the straight man who should do the feeding.

Max Wall had a still longer experience of the halls behind him when he played Vladimir. He had performed for years as acrobat and comic dancer before expanding into speaking roles in pantomime and wartime radio comedy and then in the mid-forties becoming celebrated as a solo comedian with a style entirely his own. His act included a wonderful turn with a manic Professor and a piano, in the course of which he called for a stool in a long drawn out gurgle, 'Stoo-oo-l' — a curious anticipation of Beckett's Krapp, similarly relishing the word 'Spool'. The coincidence was appropriate, for after moving into serious drama in a performance of *Ubu Roi*, Wall advanced to Beckett and did actually play Krapp, at the Greenwich Theatre in 1975 (later he appeared in David Clark's remake of *Film*, taking the role originally played by Buster Keaton). By the time he came to *Godot*, he thus had a very good idea of how Beckett's ping-pong games differed from those of music-hall as well as how they resembled them. He tailored his comedian's style, eschewing its more manic and mocking aspects and bringing out a dignity that was a notable feature of his interpretation. 'Man's dignity and the loss of it' seemed to him one of

Beckett's abiding concerns. He and Trevor Peacock, playing Estragon, made a good pair, contrasting physically in that Wall was the lighter, somewhat frailer of the two and Peacock, dark, heavier, more robust: a contrast fitting the emphasis in the text on Estragon's earthiness and Vladimir's mental agility.

Didi and Gogo, to use the names they always use to each other, were from the start a music-hall pair, with Gogo as the straight man, though as Irving Wardle pointed out,[13] the straight man who got the laughs, when he bungled a routine like the hat juggling, for instance. They wore the ubiquitous bowler hats but Didi's superior status was hinted at in his shabby genteel costume, camel hair coat with velvet collar and pinned-on bow tie, all mangy but redolent of better days. The costume took a turn towards music-hall in the slap shoes and pinstripe trousers, immensely wide at the bottom to allow for the spread-out gait just teetering on the edge of the absurd. This walk was one of Wall's specialities in his music-hall act. Here, it was never allowed to go over the top. Those hasty exits for a necessary purpose were funny but not so funny that they prevented us from remembering they really were necessary. Gogo's 'End of the corridor, on the left' got its laugh but there was no pressure to go on laughing when Didi came back, '*sombre*', as the text requires. Peacock was the more dilapidated of the pair in a vest with great gaping holes, tattered jacket and baggy trousers gathered in at the big boots. He seemed to carry the marks of those rough times sleeping in ditches and being beaten up by nameless gangs, and he had a kind of helplessness in the face of it all which convincingly coexisted with his robust, high spirited game-playing with Didi. He could not be pinned down simply as the straight man. This was a Gogo easily capable of the flights into his partner's mode which the text calls for. It was with characteristic vigour that '*aphoristic for once*', he responded to Didi's peroration on the 'abysmal depths' [p. 80]: 'We are all born mad. Some remain so.'

These two were not just partners but companions, lost at the 'crossroads of life' as Max Wall saw it: theirs was a close relationship based on character and need. A great strength of Wall's performance was the genuine clown's melancholy behind the comic features, the mobile eyebrows, the deceptively soft, insinuating voice and the large mouth that could shut like a trap as the head thrust itself forward. He was a natural thinker and brooder, Gogo more of a fighter. Their opening scene established the pattern of an extremely human relationship. Gogo struggling with the recalcitrant boot was not gloomily resigned. His 'Nothing to be done' was more like a stage in the battle, a moment of impasse not defeat. Wall's Didi had an equally solid assurance in its own way. He came on alert and attentive, picking up Gogo's thought with 'I'm beginning to come round to that opinion'. Then he abstracted himself, perfectly catching the half-serious, half-mocking style hinted at in the text:

> All my life I've tried to put it from me, saying, Vladimir, be reasonable, you haven't yet tried everything. And I resumed the struggle. (*He broods, musing on the struggle.*)
>
> [p. 9]

This talking to himself, with just a touch of self-mockery ('*musing on the struggle*') came over with great naturalness, as did the many pauses in which he gave himself time to think. Wall has said that he feels an affinity with Beckett, is at ease with his solitaries, being a loner himself in life as well as in his career as a solo performer. He understands the technique of pauses, having used something like it in his own music-hall routines. He would indulge in a long pause, gazing into space and keeping the audience waiting beyond the norm, then apologise, 'Excuse me, I was miles away'. It was a comedian's pause, for a laugh, but the technique came easily, Wall implies, because it was natural for him in life to withdraw himself in just such a way. Braham Murray's direction made good use of this propensity. The withdrawals into musing which, as we noticed earlier, may sometimes seem inconsequential to a reader, in Wall's performance seemed the most natural thing in the world:

VLADIMIR: . . . Never neglect the little things of life.
ESTRAGON: What do you expect, you always wait till the last moment.

VLADIMIR:      (*musingly*). The last moment . . . (*He meditates.*)
               Hope deferred maketh the something sick,
               who said that?
ESTRAGON:      Why don't you help me?
VLADIMIR:      Sometimes I feel it coming all the same.
               Then I go all queer.

[p. 10]

At that moment, one felt, Didi was so taken up with defining
his attitude to the concept of hope that he was simply
unaware of Gogo's call for help. It was a pattern that
became familiar: Gogo with his mind on the near and
immediate, Didi prone to abstract himself into the world of
reflection. Wall handled the crossed-line effects that
resulted from these divergencies with the ease of a seasoned
comedian but they never became merely comic crosstalk.
They were glimpses into a genuine meditative process for
which Peacock's Gogo had a kind of baffled sympathy which
easily turned to impatience. He had a quick intelligence of
his own, enjoyed games and mock battles and returned the
ball vigorously when it fell squarely in his court: lines like
'That's the idea, let's abuse each other' were delivered with
great gusto. But he was wary of philosophising. When he
surprised us by coming out with his large aphorism — 'We
are all born mad. Some remain so.' — we knew it would not
be long before he came down to earth again. So it was; in the
next breath he was giving his mind to fallen Pozzo's offer of
payment for help (Didi, meanwhile, still brooding on the
aphorism):

ESTRAGON:      (*aphoristic for once*). We are all born mad. Some
               remain so.
POZZO:         Help! I'll pay you!
ESTRAGON:      How much?
POZZO:         One hundred francs!
ESTRAGON:      It's not enough.
VLADIMIR:      I wouldn't go so far as that.
ESTRAGON:      You think it's enough?
VLADIMIR:      No, I mean so far as to assert that I was weak
               in the head when I came into the world. But
               that is not the question.

[p. 80]

This time the reflective process led into a decision to take action and give Pozzo a helping hand. Commentators have observed that many cries for help go unheeded in the play: a moral point is being made. Wall's Didi, however, came over resoundingly as the least culpable person in this respect. He did indeed turn away regularly into his inner world, and there was no question but that he could be tough. He gleefully encouraged Gogo to take his revenge on Lucky in Act 2, as if allowing him a treat. And there was often a feeling that his clown's mischief might develop into something more anarchic. Every now and then he became much larger than life, as in his high-coloured account of the tiger species [p. 80]. This gave a slightly dangerous quality to the turns. There was just a hint occasionally of the music-hall persona who used to control his audience with a kind of steely glee, having ruthless fun with latecomers, drawing us into uneasy connivance with his running joke about their possible misadventures with a motor bike. But it was also clear from his whole stance and style that this Didi was essentially a moral being with a strong sense of responsibility and a capacity to feel for others. He conveyed this without falling into the tear trap perspicaciously identified by Blin. When he broke away from abstractions, i.e. in the 'Help' scene, and moved purposefully toward Pozzo — 'Come, let's get to work!' [p. 81] — he was very much in earnest. Yet he was still, in part, the comic philosopher, with his faintly grotesque walk and his ability to find a plethora of reasons for doing the obvious. On a somewhat roguish note, he tried out different arguments on his stubborn partner from those which had earlier failed to make an impact beyond drawing the aphorism about humanity being born mad. Having once made his own mind up, he soon charmed Gogo into following suit, with the blithe ease of someone used to handling difficult audiences from a solo stance:

No, don't protest, we are bored to death, there's no denying it. Good. A diversion comes along and what do we do? We let it go to waste. Come, let's get to work!

[p. 81]

This Didi had a natural authority which stemmed from the melancholy of the clown as well as the formidable repertoire of techniques for handling people. Wall has spoken in interviews of how important it is for someone playing Beckett's characters to have had a full experience of life, with all its ups and downs, its dark and light. He has been frank in interviews about the swings of fortune and emotional states in his own long life, saying that they have given him a strong feeling of affinity with Beckett, both as man and artist. In the end, it was the force of a thinking character that dominated his portrayal of Didi. When he came out with lines like 'Thinking is not the worst' [p. 64], they conveyed a sense of real inner pain: we could see why games were needed to lighten dark abysses.

Comic, darkly ironic and sad were really at one in this production. The 'two heads for three hats' routine [p. 71] was an obvious opportunity for Wall to display his music-hall virtuosity and he seized on it to introduce a special gag, setting the hat rolling down his arm and into his hand before passing it on to Gogo. But this, like everything else was bound up with his benevolent impulse to make his partner a little happier. In the way of a silent film actor he used his whole body to cheer Gogo up; shaking his clasped hands, miming encouragement, introducing the hat game with a wealth of facial persuasiveness. As with the Laurel and Hardy pair, who preceded him in the classic routine, he knew the straight man would bungle it, but, as Wall has commented, the superior clown has a real affection, underneath all the irritation, for the one left holding the baby. His Didi exerted all his arts to coax Gogo out of his black moods. It was an almost motherly attitude to his other half: Wall saw him in fact as essentially a 'sulky child'. When Gogo mistook the fallen Pozzo for Godot he corrected him with quiet authority, as if from sad, adult knowledge, 'It's not Godot'. Or he would tempt him to be good (to stay and help Pozzo) with a wily smile and insinuating vocal note, 'Perhaps he has another bone for you'. There was just a touch of the clown's mischief about this, as in his handling of Gogo's suggestions that they should blackmail Pozzo and beat Lucky. He humoured him

— 'That seems intelligent all right' — but he was only biding his time for an agile clown's turn:

VLADIMIR:    . . . No, the best would be to take advantage
                  of Pozzo's calling for help —
POZZO:        Help!
VLADIMIR:    To help him —

[p. 79]

Wall administered the coup-de-grace, the unlooked-for conclusion, with head thrust forward and voice softly triumphant, 'To help him'. Trevor Peacock's Gogo was a strong personality in his own right but it was always clear that Didi was the leader. Just occasionally there was the hint of a faint likeness to the other pair. Wall mimicked them both with rather alarming accuracy: he seemed to draw on something he had identified in the character of Didi to give Gogo a sinister lesson in doing Pozzo, 'Think, pig!' When Gogo failed in the role, he took over both parts with brio, giving himself the Pozzo commands with the surreal aplomb of a professional ventriloquist, but responding out of his own troubled depths, 'I can't!'. Wolfe Morris as a business-like Pozzo (in city suit) and Gary Waldhorn as a chalk-faced Lucky, mouthing the think like an automaton, created solid presences for the monstrous pair. When Max Wall reflected them in his brilliant mirror, however, the divisions between the personae momentarily shifted and blurred: they were feeding into some strange whole.

Braham Murray's production brought out to the full the value of a great music-hall art such as Max Wall's to the playing of Beckett. And it interestingly established the gains to be made by performance free of the fourth wall.

17  NATIONAL THEATRE (LYTTELTON), LONDON, 1987

Alec McCowen as Vladimir, John Alderton as Estragon, Colin Welland as Pozzo, Peter Wight as Lucky, Simon

Privett/Simon Doe as A Boy. Directed by Michael Rudman.
Opened 25 November 1987.

This production could be said to have chosen itself. It is an
important recent British one which enjoyed great success
with the large and varied audiences of the National Theatre.
It was the first production of the play by the NT Company,
and the first British one to be based on the as-yet-
unpublished 'performance text', incorporating revisions
made by Beckett for the 1975 Schiller-Theater production
and the 1984 production by the San Quentin Drama
Workshop. Walter Asmus, who worked with Beckett in
West Berlin and with Rick Cluchey's company in Chicago
before they came to the Riverside Studios London for their
ten days with Beckett, also gave advice on Michael
Rudman's production. It is therefore a production with a
significant place in the complex stage history of the play.

It is a curious situation when a production has claim to be
more definitive than the text currently so approved by its
author. This is not the place for an exhaustive analysis of
the textual changes which can be observed in it. Some have
been touched on already in the course of discussion and this
seems the best way to continue. However, the question
must be asked at the start: how far would the changes
incorporated in Michael Rudman's production be likely to
strike members of the audience who were not Beckett
scholars but were reasonably familiar with the 1965 text?

Answers to that question would obviously vary, as no
doubt would views on the desirability or otherwise of the
changes. The revisions most people would probably notice
are those to do with the presentation of Pozzo. In Act 1, for
instance, he no longer has the pipe routine [p. 28] which at
the Royal Exchange, as in other early productions, added a
layer of histrionic exhibitionism to his character. Beckett
had come to find it extraneous. So too with the long
sequence in Act 2 [pp. 85–6] when Pozzo has been helped
to his feet by Vladimir and Estragon and is held sagging
between them while they conduct a leisurely conversation
about the evening and the approach of night. None of this
was heard in the National Theatre production. Instead, the

actors moved straight from Pozzo's 'I used to have wonderful sight' to Estragon's 'Expand! Expand!', and then to Vladimir's comment, that Pozzo is thinking of happier days.

Such cuts were made in the cause of tightening up the text and preventing loss of rhythmic momentum. However, as Colin Duckworth has noted,[14] the overall playing time was extended, not decreased in Beckett's own productions, from two hours to three. Michael Rudman did not follow Beckett in that respect: allowing for the interval, his production ran for barely two hours. He did not use space that might have been provided by the cuts (additions take up little room) to lengthen pauses and tableaux in the manner of the Schiller-Theater or San Quentin Drama Workshop productions. The slowing down Beckett favours — an aspect of his theatre that brings to mind the mystical slowness of Japanese Noh — was no more a feature of Rudman's production than it had been of Peter Hall's thirty years earlier. For English audiences, it seems, a somewhat brisker movement is found safer. Michael Rudman has indeed said that 'only a production rooted in naturalism will work in Britain' (a comment to which we will return later).

What the production brought out most purposefully were those moments of symbolic grouping which Beckett stresses in his Production Notebook. The deletion of the evening sequence discussed above did in fact allow for a bolder, more concentrated visual effect. The tableau of the raised-up Pozzo, supported by the other two and drooping between them, had more iconic force as an image when not dissipated by the long conversation; a further cut, of all the references to the Board, sharpened the effect still further. The image worked as it was clearly meant to, carrying an echo from the similar tableau in Act 1 when the actors raised Lucky from the fall following the think and supported him between them an instant, before letting him drop.

It was iconography of the Fall and of the Crucifixion all in one, a full scenic realisation of those motifs which could be said to dominate the play. Of course these particular tableaux already exist in the text; simply, they were made to stand out more sharply in the NT production by observance of the clearing that Beckett's revisions had created. Other symbolic groupings would have been more surprising to someone familiar with the text but not with Beckett's directorial additions. One such was the moment in the game-playing of Act 2, just before the entry of Pozzo and Lucky. Vladimir, staggering about as the text requires, placed himself against the tree with arms flung out so as to make the shape of a cross, yet another silent reminder of the theme he had voiced at the start of the play, 'Two thieves, crucified at the same time as our Saviour'. Another surprise moment for our hypothetical member of the audience would have been the wonderfully light-hearted episode when Didi and Gogo (to revert to their stage names) waltzed about the stage, humming the tune of the Merry Widow Waltz and making up after their duel of insults. This reconciliation waltz was part of a musical pattern in Act 2 (Act 1 has no music) which insinuated concepts as well as feeling into the play. The waltz round, as Dougald McMillan has pointed out[15] picks up the shape of Didi's song at the start of the act, the song that need never come to an end, being structured to go round in a circle. Thus, large concepts such as the circularity of time were reinforced by this little outburst of frivolity.

The frivolity was also welcome in itself, a moment of pure pleasure and rest from reflection. The actors seized on it as such; they clearly relished the opportunity to give the audience a surprise treat. All the musical openings were taken with gusto: Didi's dog song, the lullaby he sings to Gogo (comedy uppermost here, though it shaded off into more poignant, nursery style quietness) and the funeral march hummed when Didi walks Gogo about the stage to shake off his nightmare. In this too, comic incongruity was dominant; the nightmare receded rather easily.

What changes other than these striking scenic and musical ones — and the cuts touched on earlier — would force themselves on attention without aid of footnotes? Wording changes are more difficult for a reader to register in the course of a production but some of these too would surely stand out, perhaps causing a little shock of loss. It is always disconcerting to lose familiar lines from a well-loved text (Colin Duckworth has expressed strong views about this). Some would surely have missed the humour of the original when Gogo answered Pozzo's question about Didi's age with 'Ageless' instead of 'Eleven', while the rigorous cutting of Pozzo's scenes — the vapouriser, the second pipe routine and so forth [pp. 28–9] — deprived him of some memorable lines. The NT Pozzo no longer said 'He refused once' nor ruminated, 'I am not perhaps particularly human, but who cares?'. The characterisation discussed in the first section took on a slightly different look at times as a result of these line changes.

Although in a text of such fine precision every word or pause counts, the more minute textual changes might well have passed unnoticed or made no more than a faint impact in the course of the performance. Yet the fresh, invigorating quality of the production owed much to the impression of newness — a word here, a phrase there, or a small chunk of dialogue. It might be some tiny change that would be noticed, like the correction of Pozzo's inaccurate description of Atlas as 'son of Jupiter'. Or a more noticeable and crucial one, the addition of 'Yes!' to Gogo's repeated 'Ah' (a change we will return to). Good readers of the text would certainly have spotted the changed form of Didi's question to the Boy about the colour of Godot's beard. It was now 'Fair or . . . or black . . . or red?', 'red' being an addition which, as Ruby Cohn has pointed out[17] relates back to the story in Act 1 about the Englishman in the brothel, thus linking the bawdy and the metaphysical in a curious way.

Turning now to the production as a whole, the first striking thing about it was its unusual set. Whereas in the Royal Exchange production it was the theatre space itself, a stage in the midst of a vast foyer, that made the impact, here, at the Lyttelton, the space was conventional, a proscenium theatre such as the play has often been performed in. Decidedly unexpected, however, was the elaborate setting (designed by William Dudley). The country road that, in Beckett's own production, was nothing but stage floor, had become a space at the foot of a steep, irregularly sloping, pitted, grey bank, rising to a highroad in the background; a real traffic road, with white lines and the look of going somewhere. The effect was interesting but distracting. It obviously allowed the actors more varied movement than the undifferentiated flat stage of Beckett's preference, and they were very busy on it indeed. Pozzo and Lucky made their entrance down and across the ridge, a move which somewhat masked the purposefulness of their straight line, since the bank was capacious, allowing room for straying in various directions. The sense of enclosure was still there (the 'lunar cavity', as one reviewer saw it, was not easy to negotiate) but it had been diminished. This void had more in it to distract attention from voidness, so it was easier for the characters to give themselves the illusion of occupation and for the audience to get relief from the dread pressure of emptiness. It was said that people attending the very first productions of the play sometimes left after the interval when they realised that they were being confronted by the same set, with its uncompromising refusal of variety. The setting in the NT production cut out some of that deliberate monotony simply by offering the actors chances to vary movements and groupings. Gogo took Pozzo up the bank for a better view of Didi relieving himself off-stage; Didi and Gogo climbed to the top of the ridge for their battle of insults (more than ever like a comic duel, exposed on that high ground) and came down again for their spirited reconciliation waltz on the foreground stage. And so on. Probably the variety made possible by this set was one of the elements, along with the swifter rhythm already mentioned, making for the audience's happiness with the production. If to succeed in Britain, as Michael Rudman suggested, a production 'must be rooted in naturalism', this setting had enough of naturalism in it (despite the moon crater effect) to provide an appropriate environment for a performance the audiences at the Lyttelton could expect to enjoy.

What kind of performance was that, and how did it shape our idea of the play? Above all, it was based on character. These were solidly real people, Peter Wight's Lucky included (his rendering of the think was remarkable for its calculated approximation to reasonableness). The greater ordinariness of these personae showed straightaway in their costume. Battered and dishevelled though it was, it had not gone all the way to trampdom nor were the pairs teamed up in complementary checks and colours in a way that stressed pattern or hinted at circus or music-hall. (Beckett had moved away from vaudevillian emphases at the time he worked with the San Quentin actors, according to their report, so the merely shabby look of the NT actors might have pleased him. On the other hand, his Pozzo had become progressively more seedy, with holed trousers, hardly distinguishable in that respect from Gogo and Didi and casting grave doubt on his ownership of a Steinway, a late addition to his off-stage possessions.) Colin Welland's Pozzo in the NT production was no tramp but a comfortable country gentleman in his brown striped suit and felt hat, nearer to what the character claims to be. There was an emphatic contrast with Didi, in his old frock coat and flannel trousers, cardigan-style waistcoat and stove-pipe top hat, and Gogo in worn jacket and open-necked shirt (and tough boots). Lucky belonged with them, so far as costume went; his grey flannels and fawn jacket were unexceptional, shabbily conventional wear.

In these more ordinary clothes the actors created characters with whom the audience were invited to feel at home. It really was a sort of home that Didi and Gogo had made there, in their strange burrow under the highroad, like the creatures in *The Wind in the Willows* (rather a passport to English affections). The tender relationship between them fitted easily into this scheme of things, including the touch of nursemaid in Alec McCowen's soothing attitude to his partner. Interestingly, it was John Alderton, celebrated for his very funny performances in P. G. Wodehouse and other comic roles and a founder member of the Theatre of Comedy, who played Estragon (at Manchester the role of the straight-man), while Alec McCowen, known among much else for his one-man readings of St Mark's Gospel, who played Vladimir, the Max Wall role at the Royal Exchange. They made the characters their own with seeming ease, bringing out once again the richness of the parts and the way they can yield up somewhat different facets to the different personalities of the actors handling them.

These personalities were established in the first minute or two after their entrances and made a striking contrast. Didi was the lightweight, perpetually dancing about, sometimes on the spot, in a way that reminded of his urinary trouble but also seemed an indication of something flighty about him. Gogo was the heavy man, dark and full of inner tension, but droll in a dry, down-to-earth style that gave the impression (as did Didi's jauntiness) of being basic to his character, not a variety turn. He sat on his stone (an important feature of the set) as if he really needed to, taking up the restful foetal posture whenever he could, while Didi bobbed around, restless, unable to keep still for long. They conveyed the impression that their game-playing and other exchanges sprang from temperament; they would have been like this anywhere. So in Act 2, after discussing the puzzle of the boots — are they Gogo's or not? — McCowen showed an impish pleasure in switching from one diversion to another: first, the solace of radishes or carrots, then the idea of trying on the boots (Gogo a step behind, still thinking about vegetables):

| | |
|---|---|
| VLADIMIR: | What about trying them? |
| ESTRAGON: | I've tried everything. |
| VLADIMIR: | No, I mean the boots. |
| ESTRAGON: | Would that be a good thing? |
| VLADIMIR: | It'd pass the time. (*Estragon hesitates.*) I assure you, it'd be an occupation. |
| ESTRAGON: | A relaxation. |
| VLADIMIR: | A recreation. |
| ESTRAGON: | A relaxation. |
| VLADIMIR: | Try. |
| ESTRAGON: | You'll help me? |
| VLADIMIR: | I will of course. |
| ESTRAGON: | We don't manage too badly, eh Didi, between the two of us? |
| VLADIMIR: | Yes yes. Come on, we'll try the left first. |
| ESTRAGON: | We always find something, eh Didi, to give us the impression we exist? |

[pp. 68–9]

John Alderton communicated the hesitation called for here through one of the darkly reserved looks that was a mark of his style. This Gogo always seemed to have a subterranean life of feeling which might at any time erupt into passion. Without losing the frolicsome swing of the rhythm he managed to suggest, by musing emphasis on his term 'relaxation', that it was no idle choice of word but represented a real need for him. There was a faint hint too in his questioning of Didi that he might not be so much taken up with the existential issue ('the impression we exist?') as putting off the evil hour when he would have to try on the painful boots. McCowen's practical, lightsome Didi seemed to have some such suspicion, brushing aside the large thought and concentrating on the need for action: 'Yes yes, we're magicians. But let us persevere in what we have resolved, before we forget'. The boot-trying routine was a real jaunt, a kind of comic dance about the stage, Gogo supported by Didi, his foot high in the air, Didi mimicking Pozzo — 'The other, hog!' — and everyone, including the audience, having great fun. The strength of Alderton's performance showed at the end of the routine when he cut off further talk about the boots with an 'Enough!' that came from some painful place within. This was not a Gogo to be trifled with. Even in his silences he was always at full stretch: it was easy to understand why he would find sleep difficult. When he took up his foetal posture on the stone, head between the knees, it could be thought that he had retreated into some stormy consciousness where Didi did not go. Didi's role was to watch over his partner, spread his own coat over the shoulders of the sleeping man and then walk about to keep himself warm, his restlessness given a purpose born of affection.

This was almost the reverse of the Wall/Peacock relationship, where Didi had the greater weight as superior intelligence and magician. McCowen and Alderton were more equal in the performance line. Gogo had his streak of mischief: he enjoyed himself miming Didi's movements when he was off-stage relieving himself and he quite held his own in the hat-passing routine. In tune with the prevailing interest of the production in character the routine was embellished by mimicry, which brought the missing hat-owner Lucky into the scene. The pair did an exaggerated version of his style; vacant, ecstatic look, eyes rolling up to heaven.

Always there was this sense of a human rationale, behind even the most farcical or fantastic episodes, for instance, walking to the funeral march to shake off the nightmare. The funeral march certainly struck a note of universality with its melancholy intimations of mortality but the emotional focus was on Gogo's nightmare, his terror of falling. Alderton made the character so interesting that we were ready to be involved in anything he was experiencing (unlike Didi who can't bear to hear about his dreams — 'Don't tell me!'). His 'Ah yes!' at the end of each 'We're waiting for Godot' sequence was a highly expressive sound, half humorous, half desperate, loaded with the sort of meaning Beckett himself brought to it when he tried the sound of 'Ah, yes!' instead of 'Ah!' for the San Quentin actors. It was the voice of rueful experience: 'Still the same old thing, still the same old thing'. This was a valuable revision for the production, giving Alderton scope for his interpretation of Gogo as a by-no-means simple soul. In this partnership it was, if anything, Vladimir who seemed the less complex of the two; though the more agile and mercurial, he gave the impression of having fewer depths and reserves. Or perhaps he was simply more controlled. His outburst, 'Christ have mercy on us!', in the last scene with the Boy had not the same feeling of panicky grief as Gogo's similar outbreak, 'What'll we do?'.

The strong impression of human links and likenesses between these opposite beings was extended in a striking way to the other pair. Colin Welland's Pozzo was pompous and comfortable rather than a ringmaster or the 'overbearing landowner' Beckett told the San Quentin actors he wanted to abandon. Partly as a result of losing some threatening lines like 'He refused once', and some routines, including the whip-cracking preparation for the 'twilight' speech in Act 1, this Pozzo was rather less sinister, less outrageously histrionic than some have been. The effect fitted in well with the general humanising that was a mark of the production. It was appropriate, one felt, that this Pozzo should no longer say, 'I am not particularly human, but who cares?' He was sinister enough still in his fleshly, jovial way; a big man, rotund and flamboyant; his bullying had an alarmingly matter-of-fact quality.

His other half, Lucky, came as close to ordinariness as would be possible for a character obliged to stand with a rope round his neck carrying bags he can never put down except on command. No drooling puppet nor white-faced clown, this; he was startlingly real, commonplace in dress (the grey flannels, the fawn jacket with the leather elbow patches) and with a kind of dull pleasantness of expression, except when he turned nasty as it was obvious he easily could. He was like one fallen on bad times who was still attached, grotesquely, to the world of hampers, chicken and wine and odes to evening. Pozzo possessed him but he shot his own possessive glances in his master's direction. It was easier than it often is with this character to believe in the handy-andy symbiosis Pozzo notes for us: 'Remark that I might just as well have been in his shoes and he in mine'. The dance in Peter Wight's rendering gave an interesting impression of being carefully thought out, a difficult, clumsy balancing act, as of one trying to dance in a too-narrow space. The title Pozzo supplied seemed right: 'The Net. He thinks he's entangled in a net'. At its conclusion he folded up, crouching so low he seemed almost to have fallen, then awkwardly recovered himself and went into the encore with a kind of complacency. He was a man who liked to perform, even in such a humiliating context.

Just the same impression was created by the think. This was one of the most startling surprises of the production. Peter Wight delivered it in a calmly pleased, assured way, not as nonsense pouring out from an automaton but as an argument whose merits would be appreciated and points taken. The fact that it sometimes went off into bizarre parody — 'a personal God quaquaquaqua with white beard quaquaquaqua outside time without extension' — curiously did not prevent it from being serious. Rather, he seemed to be giving us the complete unedited version of his thoughts, including outbursts of irritation, scepticism, mental jeers, and confusions. When he held up the flow, the maddening stops and starts to which it was helplessly subject suggested a recognisable kind of pedantry; these were fussy corrections or attempts to keep the headlong argument in control:

> . . . it is established beyond all doubt all other doubt than that which clings to the labours of men that as a result of the labours unfinished of Testew and Cunard it is established as hereinafter but not so fast for reasons unknown . . .'
>
> [p. 43]

Beckett had aimed to 'give confusion a shape'. As Michael Rudman directed Lucky this aim was kept in view. Probably for the first time in many British theatre-goers' experience the think emerged as something to be followed (if with difficulty). Like the edge of pavements in a fog, there could just be glimpsed the sort of pattern Beckett himself had traced when directing the Schiller company. Perhaps in this production, in tune with its whole state, more interest was invited for the character of Lucky. There was a congruity between the reasonable delivery of the speech and his appearance: the ruined academic, with his leather patches and the trailing grey hair he was forced by his master to reveal to show how much younger the sixty-year old Pozzo looked. Pozzo incidentally was not 'completely bald' as the text says, but well furnished with hair to match his generally well oiled look.

In its weaving of the many elements that make the play so complex, the production gave full value to characterisation, rather less to the lyrical and mystical. When Gogo looked up at the moon and murmured 'Pale for weariness' he gave the lyrical moment little force, hurrying on to the dry anti-climax, 'Of climbing heaven and gazing on the likes of us.' Certainly there appeared to be directorial intention to mark the lyricism of the haunting scene in Act 2 [p. 63] when the 'dead voices' are heard. The actors showed their awareness of the changed mood by dropping their wry jauntiness for a more charged vocal tone. They added movements, walking away upstage, standing with backs to audience as if trying to conceal the emotion that was threatening their customary aplomb. The lyricism did not fully develop, however. The music of the voices rustling in the leaves, evoking a life that was gone, was there for the sake of the characters rather than for itself. At such a moment one felt the need for a slower rhythm, to capture the visionary stillness of the scene.

Stillness of some potency however descended at the end of each act with the coming of the moon. The embankment setting came into its own here. It had proved distracting for the appearances of the Boy, which were less affecting than in the Royal Exchange production. Naturalism ran into difficulties with the enigmatic simplicity of those epiphanies. But the dream-like atmosphere was captured when the pale moon came up, faintly irradiating the pitted bank, turning it into a lunar surface with a dimension of poetic mystery. In this more ethereal setting the suicide business with the rope and the trousers took on gravity, without the actors needing to change from their easy, conversational tone. They discussed the melancholy plan — 'Why don't we hang ourselves?' — with the practical interest they had brought to all their efforts to fill in time. By now it seemed utterly characteristic that Gogo should come nearest to breaking down ('I can't go on like this') and Didi bring him back into order with the sardonic, 'That's what you think' and the amused command, 'Pull ON your trousers', which effectively waved suicide goodbye.

The so-different productions that have been discussed surely demonstrate above all the versatility of Beckett's play. Although his own production must stand out for those who saw it as incomparable, this is not to say that other interpretations become invalid. If that were so, if there were only one way of doing the play, it would presumably cease to be done: the creativity of theatre artists would find no place. But even when all the detail of Beckett's directorial thinking becomes universally known there will be room, one must believe, for new approaches. *Waiting for Godot* is a play that calls out individualism, in the reactions of audiences as well as in the interpretations of directors, actors and designers. It is a world where we will always be able to see new things.

*Happy Days*

## 18   Note on the Schiller-Theater Werkstatt West Berlin 1971 Production

The first production of *Happy Days*, directed by Alan
Schneider, was at the Cherry Lane Theatre, New York (17
September 1961) with Ruth White as Winnie. Ten years
later Beckett directed the German version of the play
himself, at the Schiller-Theater Werkstatt (the smaller,
studio theatre of the Schiller company) with Eva Katharina
Schultz as Winnie. His Regiebuch was published, the
Schiller notebooks were deposited in the Samuel Beckett
Archive at Reading University (as, later the English
Production Notebook) and there have been detailed
accounts of the rehearsal process by Ruby Cohn (in *Back to
Beckett*) and others. In 1979 Beckett directed the play in
English (its original language) at the Royal Court Theatre,
with Billie Whitelaw as Winnie. His Production Notebook,
edited by James Knowlson, was published in 1985. There is
therefore a large body of material available for those
wishing to know how the author saw the play when he
directed it on different occasions.

As with *Waiting for Godot*, it has not been easy to select two
from the many brilliant performances that have been given.
I have chosen to focus on Peter Hall's production at the
National Theatre, London in 1975, with Peggy Ashcroft as
Winnie, and on Beckett's own production at the Royal
Court Theatre, London in 1979, with Billie Whitelaw. They
were both fascinating performances in almost opposite
styles; a further demonstration of how Beckett's plays can
lend themselves (within limits) to individual approaches, in
the process revealing different facets of their complex form.
I will begin, however, with a brief word on the German
production which gave particularly full insights into Beckett's own view of the play.

When he directed *Happy Days* at the Schiller-Theater
Werkstatt, Beckett gave some very interesting advice to his
actors. As always, this was to do with the minute detail of

the performance: exactly how Willie's hand should be placed at the end when he approaches nearer to Winnie — or the revolver; how far forward Winnie should lean on different occasions, the exact posture she should take up when sleeping (significantly, one arm was to cradle her precious bag, so long as she had an arm). What kind of voice she should speak in was a crucial issue. Beckett's emphasis, in the Schiller notes, was on the contrast between Acts 1 and 2, on Winnie's ability to 'do' other voices (the Shower/ Cooker pair, Willie proposing marriage) and on the child-like notes in her chatter. The variety and colour of Act 1 depended primarily on Schultz's voice: it was to be a voice of 'many colours' in sharp contrast to the 'white voice' she was to adopt in Act 2, to match the draining away of her powers and faculties. Yet she was still to demonstrate her actress-like skills, putting on a childish voice to tell the story of Mildred and the mouse just as she puts on Willie's voice to recall him as he was.

Although the focus evidently had to be on Winnie, Beckett wanted Willie to be very much in the picture, their relationship a crucial thing. Beckett slightly modified the stage picture to this end. Instead of being in the *'exact centre of mound'* as the text specifies, Winnie was moved slightly to stage left. The *'maximum symmetry'* originally envisaged had been marginally disturbed, indicating the importance Beckett attached to the Winnie/Willie partnership (the play in draft form had at one time been called *Winnie/Willie Notes*). Like Didi and Gogo or Pozzo and Lucky, we might say, Winnie and Willie were to be seen as a pair, and like the others they formed a sharp contrast. Willie, said Beckett in his Schiller notes, was an 'old turtle', a creature of the earth, Winnie in contrast was 'air and fire'. This was a light on the character which the actress had to take into account along with the other emphases on child-like prattle and so forth: a complex combination.

The piercing bell was another important feature. Winnie had to react strongly to it: it was her enemy. Beckett also wanted the audience to be aware of the connection between her problem with time and her fragmented speech and behaviour. He gives a self-instruction in his Production

Notebook: 'Relate frequency of broken speech and action to discontinuity of time. Winnie's time experience, incomprehensible transport from one inextricable present to the next, those past unremembered, those to come inconceivable.'[18] 'Deep trouble for the mind' as Winnie says; and a trouble, we might add, common to human kind, not necessarily bound up with some deficiency in Winnie herself. Beckett's meditative note leaves that question still an open one.

## 19    NATIONAL THEATRE (LYTTELTON)/OLD VIC, LONDON, 1975/6

Peggy Ashcroft as Winnie and Alan Webb as Willie. Directed by Peter Hall. Opened at the Old Vic, 13 March 1975, transferred to Lyttelton, 1976.

Coming now to the first of my chosen British productions, I suppose the dominating impression made by Peggy Ashcroft's performance was of her warm and personal rendering of the part. This was a Winnie with an enormous fund of humorous resilience, out-going and robustly vivacious. The first English Winnie, Brenda Bruce, had seen the play as being 'about gallantry' ('I just make the best of my predicament'). Ashcroft also brought out the heroic aspect of Winnie's struggle to keep going, her good-humoured but absolute determination to control Willie and to bring herself to the point where she could sing her song. She and Hall had agreed that Winnie was 'genteel, bird-like' but that her voice should have an incantatory quality. Ashcroft also introduced a note of vocal colour Beckett had not specified, an Irish intonation, derived from her acquaintance with Beckett's own distinctively Irish tones. This persuasive, lilting sound helped to make the flow of talk seem wonderfully natural, like the seductive story-telling of Synge's Christy Mahon in *The Playboy of the Western World* which similarly acts on harsh reality, turning it into the saga of a man who murdered his own father and became the 'master of all fights'.

Beckett spent two weeks in London to advise on this production. As usual, he stressed the need for simplicity and economy. His last word to Peter Hall, on his departure, summarised his deeply-held view of art: 'All true grace is economical'. He suggested some cuts and changes in the text but only one of these was major enough to cause a shock. This was the proposal which greatly disconcerted both Ashcroft and Hall, to cut the business of the parasol burning and with it a whole page of related dialogue. Peter Hall interestingly diagnosed this proposed cut as stemming not from dissatisfaction with the text but from experience of practical difficulties 'all over the world with fire authorities and theatre technicians'.[19] The San Quentin actors observed similar reasons being given for cuts in *Godot*, as for instance on the deleted whip-cracking routine ('It never worked anyway').

In the event, the parasol episode was not cut. Peter Hall bided his time, as he said, and Peggy Ashcroft was able to retain a favourite incident which she felt the audience enjoyed for its theatricality and total unexpectedness. That was indeed its effect. It was a moment of stage audacity and danger. People laughed with pleased surprise at the sudden blaze, wondered, no doubt, how it was done, and perhaps guessed at headaches in the preparing of it. Subconsciously we may have felt that the little feat of theatrical legerdemain was an expressive symbol, in tune with Winnie's own ability to conjure up unexpected flashes from the seemingly unpromising flatness of her existence.

It was also of course a reminder of the fact that she does not control things but is subject to incomprehensible forces: the nagging bell, the heat. This last was scenically indicated by strong, unremitting light on Winnie and on the mound, which had a convincing look of scorched earth. No further suggestion of heat was made here, the ruddy tones of the cyclorama representing the receding distances of plain and sky, as the text describes. Ashcroft's feeling for the actuality of her character's experience came through in her way of reacting to her mound of earth (never sand for her, as it has sometimes been taken). The silent language in which the play is so rich, the language of movement and gesture, helped to express the complexity of that reaction, as in Act 1 where she gave her full attention to the fact that she is encased in earth:

> (*Turns back painfully front.*) The earth is very tight today, can it be I have put on flesh, I trust not. (*Pause. Absently, eyes lowered.*) The great heat possibly. (*Starts to pat and stroke ground.*) All things expanding, some more than others. (*Pause. Patting and stroking.*) Some less. (*Pause. Do.*) Oh I can well imagine what is passing through your mind . . .
>
> [p. 23]

What are these movements telling us? The opening turn of her whole body, as she moved to face front, having leaned as far back as she could, to let Willie see her, was a movement of pain: it was a statement about her bodily imprisonment. She refused to pity herself, however, coming out instead with the wonderful line about the tightness of the earth as if it were no more than a dress she were wearing. The mound was indeed seen in just that way by Edith Kern, as a kind of 'coquettish skirt' or perhaps a garment worn by an earth goddess 'whose womb and bosom are meant to enfold and nourish all'.[20] In her patting and stroking, Ashcroft conveyed a whole world of mixed feeling about this earth. She was respectful towards it, but a little possessive too; tender, almost maternal, and yet the touch suggested how strange she found it. It was as if she were recognising fully for the first time the nature of the medium in which she had her being, feeling its crumbliness, wondering about its mysterious capacities to nourish life. When later in the sequence her stroking hand touched the emmet she reacted as to an electric shock: 'Oh I say, what have we here? . . . An emmet! (*Recoils. Shrill.*) Willie, an emmet, a live emmet!' Her surprise was in the foreground but for her audience the arrival of the emmet came as a strangely inevitable climax to the long drawn out process of patting and stroking, which might almost have been seen as causing the earth to bring forth.

Peggy Ashcroft communicated some such sense: a maternal being was brooding over the inexplicable process of the creation of life in her excited observance of the emmet – 'Has like a little white ball in its arms' – and in her long silence (in which she used the magnifying glass again, then took off her spectacles and gazed before her).

The earth was also her enemy, engulfing her, as we knew it would everything. Ashcroft allowed just a hint of this sad knowledge to tinge her humorous tone when she leant back for a better view of the parasol burning behind the mound and commented, 'Ah earth you old extinguisher'. Her Winnie was a woman of vivid intuitions and rich sensibility, masked by a conventional external appearance: the commonplace, would-be smart hat with the feather, the string of pearls, the frilly decolleté and shoulder straps. In the second act, with only the unsmart hat left for adornment, she was both pathetically ordinary in a genteel way (far removed from the elegance, even in extremity, of Madeleine Renaud's Winnie). But ordinariness had by then become something extraordinary: it was heart-breaking to look at her, hear that expressive voice with its Irish lilt calling out in the tone specially used for Willie, and see the mobile face register wincingly the absence of response:

Eyes on my eyes. (*Pause.*) What is that unforgettable line? (*Pause. Eyes right.*) Willie. (*Pause. Louder.*) Willie. (*Pause. Eyes front.*) May one still speak of time? (*Pause.*) Say it is a long time now, Willie, since I saw you. (*Pause.*) Since I heard you. (*Pause.*) May one? (*Pause.*) One does. (*Smile.*) The old style! (*Smile off.*)

[p. 37]

Human feeling was uppermost here, although Ashcroft faithfully observed Beckett's direction for the switching off and on of smiles, that curious mechanical effect. Above all, this *Happy Days* was a play of character and feeling (perhaps in that sense being, like Michael Rudman's *Waiting for Godot*, rooted in naturalism despite its strong poetic charge). Winnie's relationship with Willie always came through as a crucial driving force. Hall followed Beckett's revised notion of the set, placing Winnie asymmetrically, a little to stage left, thus removing Winnie from the dead centre and making Willie's position somewhat less peripheral. The interplay between the two was strongly humorous, coloured by Ashcroft's sense of the droll. It was also powered, one felt, by a trait she drew out from Winnie's character, impatience with Willie's negativism and a deep need to counter it. She wanted his company but almost always it maddened her too.

The scene with the dirty postcard [p. 16] brought out amusingly the intimately edgy relationship they have, and could also be taken as an illustration of the crucial role of silent movements in the play. It showed Winnie thinking of Willie even when in full flow, apparently absorbed in sombre thoughts about her end ('The happy day to come when flesh melts at so many degrees'). She turned with a swooping head movement to see if he was listening properly, at which point she caught sight of his hand holding the postcard. Ashcroft's 'What is that you have there, Willie, may I see?' had, as often elsewhere, a touch of maternal watchfulness: Willie could never be trusted. There followed the droll scene in which Willie was represented only by his forearm and hand, held up throughout her talk, fingers deployed ready to snatch the card back from her. Ashcroft never lost awareness of those waiting fingers, though her irritation with them did not interfere with her determination to see the 'genuine pure filth' at close quarters (spectacles and magnifying glass came into play with the great naturalness she brought to these actions). A middle-aged lady who needed glasses was poring over an apparently pornographic postcard. This was an ironic joke, but Ashcroft made her fascination with the postcard seem not so much prurience as part of the enormous curiosity she had about everything, from God's little jokes to the writing on a toothbrush. It was typical that she soon dismissed the postcard for other thoughts (the puzzling 'hog's setae') while Willie returned to it avidly. His arm holding the card to his eyes from a variety of angles kept him very much in the picture, a dubious force, without his needing to say a word.

An interesting demonstration of taciturn Willie's importance in the play was given when John Neville took over the role (the production went to Canada but was seen with the new Willie in the Lyttelton before going there). He created a more dominating, forceful presence, someone who might well have had it in mind, as Peggy Ashcroft thought likely,[21] to kill her and then himself when he crawled towards her at the end. She had to struggle harder to maintain her identity and aspirations against his lowering presence, a struggle that brought extra danger into the play and would have provided useful material for any feminist critic in the audience. Peter Hall observed of this new relationship: '. . . it's made Winnie more vulnerable, more dependent on her hateful husband. Yet he only says 42 words from a hole under the stage. What an extraordinary thing communication in the theatre is.'[22]

The rhythm of the play and its vocal emphases were maintained in a masterful and distinctive way by Peggy Ashcroft. This was a Winnie to whom the many quotations were utterly natural. She would give a line from *Romeo and Juliet* or *Cymbeline* with just the slightest extra stress to mark it as a quotation (something Beckett had required of his German actress) but there was no division between the Winnie who prattled and sang the Merry Widow words and the Winnie who could summon up a glorious line of Yeats or Shakespeare. It was all part of the rich experience of life this Winnie had enjoyed. The sense of the richness slipping away from her, poignant in the first act, became heart-breaking in the second. When Beckett attended Hall's rehearsals he had emphasised the need to avoid overt expression of feeling, to aim at monotony, pallor and faintness.

Peter Hall knew that with Ashcroft everything must start with feeling. As an actress distinguished for so many classic roles, including the great Shakespearean ones, she knew how to bring the emotion into the austere discipline demanded by a poetic script. But she would arrive at it by way of human feeling. During the final sequence she brought her horrific experience close to us in utterly lifelike little outbursts such as, 'My neck is hurting me!', following the more exaggerated, highly-pitched scream at the climax of the Mildred story. In her final encounter with Willie, despite the awfulness of her situation, she managed to suggest through her expressive voice the fullness of the marital experience, with its shifting balance of feeling. Her maternal, nurse-like tone, 'Put on your hat, dear, it's the

sun, don't stand on ceremony, I won't mind' co-existed
easily with the faint suggestion of erotic expectation mixed
with fear and distaste: 'Is it me you're after, Willie . . . or is
it something else?'. Without strain or exaggeration, she
made the Merry Widow song, when she finally reached it,
sound as much an expression of painful ecstasy as the dying
words of Juliet or Cleopatra. We believed in it and were
moved because she had shown so much of the real, mixed
feeling that lay behind it. Her last stare at Willie, on his
knees staring at her, was the look of one who knew he might
do anything, perhaps even kill her and then himself. But she
had accepted it all. It was the most deeply moving
expression of a life lived (if not understood) to the full and
achieving a kind of dangerous consummation at its close.

20   ROYAL COURT THEATRE, LONDON, 1979

Billie Whitelaw as Winnie, Leonard Fenton as Willie.
Directed by Samuel Beckett. Opened 7 June 1979.

If Peggy Ashcroft's Winnie was close to the earth, drawing
her poetic strength from that source, Billie Whitelaw's was
a thing of air. Any Winnie is bound to seem grotesquely
trapped — the mound always has its shocking power — but
this Winnie's situation seemed strange in a more ghostly
way. Beckett wanted this emphasis on strangeness.
'Strange' (a key word in the text, as we noticed) is one of the
motifs picked out in the listed headings of his Production
Notebook and Billie Whitelaw received his recurring advice
in rehearsals to be less 'earth-bound'. She was, it seems, to
be a Winnie of air and fire, in the strongest contrast possible
to the 'old turtle' Willie, the creature of earth who eats his
own snot and never reads anything beyond the *News of the
World* at its most mundane. Leonard Fenton created a Willie
of some humorous power, out of the limited materials at his
disposal.

The setting, designed by Jocelyn Herbert, followed the by now traditional asymmetrical placing of Winnie and conveyed a potent sense of burning heat. The cyclorama opened up a prospect of flaming sky merging imperceptibly with rusty plain in a distance that seemed infinite. In this overwhelming, masterful set, Winnie lying asleep at the start of the play — her arm protecting her precious bag, her hand twitching in response to the shrill, domineering bell — was frighteningly vulnerable, an image of human fragility. Once she came awake, that impression had to be modified by the extraordinary power she in her turn began to exert over the set. Even sunk in earth so far, she kept her ability to rove and range above and beyond it. An airy lightness with something wild and alien behind it was the distinctive mark of her style. She was a soubrette, Beckett told Billie Whitelaw, and through all the variety of her discourse we never quite lost that impression. This was a younger Winnie than the character presented by Peggy Ashcroft. There was a suggestion of sexual glamour still, the pearls and the decolleté (black lace with a gleam of pink beneath, a revealing shoulder strap) belonged at least as much to the world of the lyric theatre as to middle-aged reality. The urge to song (discussed earlier as a driving force) came through irrepressibly. Beckett made a change which accentuated this effect, allowing her to sing at an earlier point in Act 2, immediately after she has evoked the scene of her long-ago wedding:

The last guest gone. (*Pause*) The last bumper with the bodies nearly touching. (*Pause.*) The look. (*Long pause.*) What day? (*Long pause.*) What look? (*Long pause.*) I hear cries. (*Pause.*) Sing. (*Pause.*) Sing your old song, Winnie.

[p. 45]

In the text she gets no further than the pause following the instruction to herself to sing before she senses Willie's arrival. Her eyes switch to the right to view him and she addresses him (in characteristically mixed terms): 'Well this is an unexpected pleasure! (*Pause.*) Reminds me of the day you came whining for my hand'. In rehearsal Beckett

changed this, directing Billie Whitelaw to begin singing
wordlessly the tune of the Merry Widow waltz, 'Though I say
not . . .' before she sees Willie (whose head showed for some
time, incongruously 'spruced', before he started his crawl:
another textual change). The earlier burst of song gave
added independence to Winnie the artist. She no longer
needed the impetus provided by Willie's crawl (as discussed
earlier) to produce her song, the song which took her above
herself like some wild, strange bird. It was now seen to have
its own source and strength, though, as Beckett noted,
Winnie's energy was in general depleted by that stage,
leaving her only bursts of vehemence.

The earlier song was one of Beckett's directorial changes
which an audience familiar with the text would pick up from
the performance with a little shock of surprise, and there
were others of a similar sort. It made a difference in one's
response, for instance, to see Willie's head first appearing,
as in the text [p. 13] *without* the blood trickling from it (the
result of Winnie's careless disposal of her empty medicine
bottle). This was a less violent introduction of the relationship between them. Another significant change was Willie's
final appearance, slumped exhausted on the mound ('flops
and lies flat' is Beckett's note), perhaps hardly capable of
reaching the revolver at all, if that was indeed his intention.
More minute changes might not have been consciously
observed, though they would surely make their mark, in a
structure where every movement of a head or a hand has
meaning. Fortunately for students of the play who want to
know the full range of the cuts and other changes made
during the Royal Court rehearsals, they have been recorded
by James Knowlson in his generously annotated edition of
Beckett's Production Notebook, the first of these Notebooks
(in English) to be published. Like all critics writing on the
play, I am indebted to this edition for the close detail it
provides of the rehearsal process. It can be seen that
Beckett rings fine changes on his own text, sometimes
causing us to modify, however slightly (as in the earlier start
to Winnie's song), interpretations based on the published
text alone. This is a point, one would hope, which the

format of this volume helps to make clear.

I want now to return to the effect of the production as a whole and to stress the qualities that made it so uniquely searching and satisfying, a transcendent experience. Above all, it worked through a rhythm of such delicacy and precision that it changed the rhythm of the watcher, in the way that Japanese Noh so famously does. Once that rhythm had established itself, even restless observers would have ceased to crave happenings more exciting than Winnie's fingering of a strand of hair or struggling to remember a line of verse. We were slowed down and held in this other dimension where everything had acquired inward significance. It was a mysterious tune that was being played through the actress, an expressive melody which allowed her many changes of tone (Beckett's Notebook interestingly registers her different 'voices') but always maintained a context of dreamlike strangeness. Billie Whitelaw's vocal modulations were timed with the exactness of an orchestral instrument. They had been rehearsed under Beckett's strict 'conducting' with just the stringency suggested in those textual directions we observed earlier. Pauses and silences were timed as carefully as the duration of the commanding bell (reduced for performance, incidentally, to between one and two seconds).

The metronome principle, so to call it, is not one all actresses could work by. It was possible for Billie Whitelaw because she was so much in tune with Beckett, had so finely intuitive an understanding of what he was aiming at in performance. Her subtle changes of vocal tone delicately rendered the movements traced in the text from one mode of feeling (or imagination) to another, as in the passage beginning 'My first ball!' [p. 15]. Whitelaw's Winnie had a dry, half humorous note in her romantic reminiscences of 'Mr Johnson, or Johnston, or perhaps I should say John*stone*' from whom she received her first kiss. She was quizzical and meditative as she reflected on the odd siting of the event, in a toolshed ('We had no toolshed and he most certainly had no toolshed'). And then, with a drop in tone which suggested that she was moving deeper into the recesses of her mind, she gave herself up to evoking the toolshed, bringing it before the mind's eye, charged with emotional atmosphere:

> (*Closes eyes.*) I see the piles of pots. (*Pauses.*) The tangles of bast. (*Pause.*) The shadows deepening among the rafters.
> [p. 15]

It was a 'brief dream', the phrase Beckett uses in his Production Notebook for such moments of reverie and which Whitelaw communicated to us as a state of mind both separate from her more earthbound moments and at the same time inextricably woven up with them; a strange phenomenon. The last of these brief dreams registered in Beckett's Notebook is when Winnie handles the revolver [p. 34]: 'Never any change. (*Pause.*) And more and more strange'. Billie Whitelaw brought this out with a kind of tranced suspension of her 'normal' self, the self that gives crawling instructions to Willie or examines the physical state of things.

One of the most striking aspects of the production was its tenuous, dreamlike balance between the level, faint, monotonous tone Beckett required and the colour, changes of perspective, bursts of energy and vivacity which are also in the play. Whitelaw contrived to introduce vocal variety without ever losing the dream feeling. She was slightly detached and distant from ordinary life even when conjuring up ordinariness in moments of sharp humour, imitating Willie's 'whine' or summoning up those philistine passers by, the Shower/Cooker pair. As she 'did' them, in Cockney voice, they seemed both vividly real and also figments from an utterly distant world, functioning on some quite other level of being. Beckett was especially pleased with this evocation, presumably not just because the Cockney mimicry was so effective but because it achieved effectiveness without going anywhere near total realism.

In the course of all these musings and dreams, Whitelaw convinced us that despite her breathless chatter, her inability to follow up an idea for long, she was someone who had an intuitive understanding of much that happened to her or might happen. She had her own kind of rationality, more scatty but not less perspicacious than the male variety. She was speaking from a wider as well as a stranger perspective when she mused to Willie on a curious sensation she experienced: '. . . some day the earth will yield and let me go, the pull is so great, yes, crack all round me and let me out' [p. 26]. She knew well enough, really, that there would be no response from him to her question 'Don't you have to cling on sometimes, Willie?' In her changed tone following his silence, there was a note of humorous recognition of the gulf she sometimes tried to pretend did not exist: 'Ah well, natural laws, natural laws, I suppose it's like everything else, it all depends on the creature you happen to be'.

There was also something wild, even manic, about this Winnie, as the text tells there has to be. Her shriek as she concluded the Mildred story was a moment of real terror, something like the awful shriek through which the same actress expressed the trauma of Mouth in the purgatorial void of *Not I*. It gave a force to the Mildred episode which took us deep into some unacknowledged hysteria of Winnie's. We could not but have it in mind when she came to her last encounter with Willie and said, with a touch of the Mildred panic, 'Don't look at me like that!'. What the trauma was we could not know, only speculate on. This was a dark note shadowing everything that followed.

When the second act opened, the dream Winnie was caught in had become tragic. This was instantly conveyed in the silent opening image; the bird-like 'soubrette' was trapped up to her neck, deprived of all external resources, mocked by the nearness of the revolver she could not use. The long-sustained silence before Winnie spoke was a necessity for this fearful image to be fully registered. Billie Whitelaw's great staring eyes in a white, drained face, spoke of an almost unbearable reduction. This was a ghost, yet she still had human feelings she was obliged to recall, like the 'dead voices' of *Waiting for Godot* ('To have lived is not enough for them.' 'They have to speak of it.') In that long-held silence, as she gazed out unseeingly, the audience waited for first words they knew could only be strange ones in this strangest of situations. It would have been hard to feel any mirth, however muted and satirical, when Whitelaw spoke (neutrally, eyes sombre) Milton's mighty invocation: 'Hail, holy light'. If this was absurd, it was an absurdity that had passed into a tragic dimension. So, too, with her response to the second bell which brutally prevents her from lapsing into unconsciousness (Beckett wanted it to cut like a knife). Whitelaw's haunted eyes set the mood: she was recalled to life and must make the best of it. 'Someone is looking at me still. (*Pause.*) Caring for me still. (*Pause.*)' Perhaps in those pauses we may have reflected on whatever beliefs we ourselves held; whether we thought it possible for a divine or other force to be controlling our existence — and our extinction.

Throughout the final act such thoughts hung in the atmosphere, giving solemnity to everything, catching up into the ghostly sense of 'ending' all the little items of Winnie's straying thought; the bag, still there, though 'blurred', the story and the memory of Willie reading titbits from *Reynolds' News*. Whitelaw maintained human feeling and humour in these reflections within a voice which insisted more than ever on its distance from reality. Its level tone, its refusal of bold emphases, its tranced quality, gave it disturbing power. Its mimicry too had become sinister; the high childish voice Whitelaw produced for the story of Mildred and the mouse was riveting in the way of a spiritualist seance. 'Eerie' was Beckett's word for the effect he wanted and this was what came through. Whitelaw's Winnie seemed at times, like her May in *Footfalls*, to be both there and not there. Her few smiles tended to be sad, her laughs mirthless, dried-up echoes. By the time she reached the final evocation of the wedding, she was far back in her mind. Willie's sudden appearance confirmed the sense of inwardness. Leonard Fenton, dapper in elegant topper, white waistcoat, white spats and the rest, was as actual as could be, down to the last detail of his pause for 'sprucing' (smoothing his moustache, dusting himself) before he advanced toward Winnie. Yet the image was never more spectral. The enormous effort needed to produce it was felt in Winnie's uncanny energy, as in the total collapse of

Willie after reaching her, with only enough drive left to stretch his hand in her direction. Or towards the revolver — Beckett preserved the ambiguity in his note 'towards W/R', with 'R' representing the revolver.

The curious, muted but driving energy reached its peak in the apotheosis of the tune played by the musical-box, that mechanical tinkling, redolent of conventional romantic dreams. When Billie Whitelaw finally sang the words all through, the quiet, uninflected voice, without straining, created an amazing effect. It was deeply poignant in a human way to hear the swaying sound of the waltz from the almost totally immobilised woman. We could tell that the tune was a mental 'prop' (the word Beckett used to describe the musical-box). The song also seemed to function on another level, where Winnie's voice was less a real voice than a sound conjured up from the past or some other space, the sound of a ghost. The same deep fusion of the human and the spectral was captured in the closing image, with Winnie's eyes opening and Willie's head raised in response to the knife-like bell and the two exchanging a long, last look. It was a tableau of absolute completeness, charged with all the complexities of thought and feeling that had been gathering throughout the production.

Beckett's own productions of his plays are uniquely compelling, as the foregoing summaries have tried to indicate. However, as I have also aimed to show, the plays are not closed but remarkably open to the different approaches that creative directors, actors and designers must necessarily take. With these plays, it is clear, text cannot ever be separated from performance. It is exciting to feel that there continues to be so much potentiality for theatrical movement and change in texts that have become so decisively recognised as modern classics.

# NOTES

1 Knowlson, J. in Cohn, R., ed., *Beckett: Waiting for Godot*, Casebook Series (London: Macmillan Education, 1987) p. 52

2 See the various studies by R. Cohn listed in the Select Reading List, including her account of the first production of *Waiting for Godot* by Roger Blin: 'Godot Cometh', in Cohn R., *From Desire to Godot: Pocket Theater of Post-war Paris* (Berkeley: University of California Press, 1987) pp. 134–80

3 States, B. O., *The Shape of Paradox* (Berkeley: University of California Press, 1978) (See Note 1, op. cit, p. 104)

4 Beckett, S. B., *Proust and Three Dialogues* (London: Calder, 1965) p. 19

5 Fletcher, J. and B. S., eds., *A Student's Guide to the Plays of Samuel Beckett* (London: Faber and Faber, rev. ed., 1985)

6 Gontarski, S. E., *The Intent of Undoing in Samuel Beckett's Dramatic Texts* (Bloomington: Indiana University Press, 1985) pp. 87

7 Quoted in Fehsenfeld, M. in *The Beckett Circle II*, Summer 1979

8 Beckett, S. B., 'Dante. . . Bruno. . . Vico. . . Joyce' in Cohn, R., ed., *Disjecta, Miscellaneous Writings and a Dramatic Fragment* (London: Calder, 1983) p. 21, p. 33

9 See Note 4, op. cit., p. 13

10 See Note 1, op. cit., p. 31

11 Hall, P. in Goodwin, J., ed., *Peter Hall's Diaries* (London: Hamish Hamilton, 1983) p. 230

12 Cohn, R., *Just Play* (New Jersey: University of Princeton Press, 1980) p. 261

13 Wardle, I., *The Times*, 14 Nov., 1980

14 Duckworth, C., 'Beckett's New *Godot*' in Acheson, J. and Arthur K., eds., *Beckett's Later Fiction and Drama* (London: Macmillan 1986) p. 184

15  See Note 1, McMillan, D. in op. cit., p.53

16  See Note 14, op. cit., p. 190

17  See Note 12, op. cit., p. 257

18  Beckett, S. B., in Knowlson, J., ed., *Happy Days. Samuel Beckett's Production Notebook*, (London: Faber and Faber, 1985) p. 150

19  See Note 11, op. cit., p. 124

20  Kern, E., *Yale French Studies*, Spring-Summer, 1962, p. 51

21  Worth, K. in Ben-Zvi, L., ed., 'Dame Peggy Ashcroft interviewed by Katharine Worth', *Women in Beckett: Gender and Genre* (Champaign: University of Illinois Press, forthcoming)

22  See Note 11, op. cit., p. 312

104

# SELECT READING LIST

Acheson, J. and Arthur, K., eds., *Beckett's Later Fiction and Drama* (London: Macmillan, 1986)
Beckett, S. B., *Waiting for Godot* (London, Faber and Faber, 1965, 2nd ed.)[+]
— *Happy Days* (London: Faber and Faber, 1966)[+]
— *Happy Days. Oh les beaux jours: a bilingual edition*, ed. J. Knowlson (London: Faber and Faber, 1978)
— *Happy Days. Samuel Beckett's Production Notebook*, ed. J. Knowlson (London: Faber and Faber, 1985)
— *The Theatrical Notebooks of Samuel Beckett, with a revised text*, general ed. J. Knowlson. In 3 vols. (London: Faber and Faber)
Vol. 1 *Waiting for Godot*, eds D. McMillan and J. Knowlson, 1990
Vol. 2 *Endgame*, ed. S. Gontarski, 1990
Vol. 3 *Krapp's Last Tape*, ed. J. Knowlson, 1990
Ben-Zvi, L., ed., *Women in Beckett: Gender and Genre* (Champaign: University of Illinois Press, forthcoming) [Includes interviews with actresses who have played Winnie in *Happy Days*]
Cohn, R., *Back to Beckett* (New Jersey: Princeton University Press, 1973)
— *Just Play* (New Jersey: University of Princeton Press, 1980)
— *From Desire to Godot: Pocket Theater of Post-war Paris* (Berkeley: University of California Press, 1987)
— ed., *Beckett: Waiting for Godot*, Casebook Series (London: Macmillan Education, 1987)
Fletcher, J. and B. S., eds, *A Student's Guide to the Plays of Samuel Beckett* (London: Faber and Faber, rev. ed., 1985)
Gontarski, S. E., *The Intent of Undoing in Samuel Beckett's Dramatic Texts* (Bloomington, Indiana University Press, 1985)

Goodwin, J., ed., *Peter Hall's Diaries* (London: Hamish Hamilton, 1983)

McMillan, D. and Fehsenfeld, M., *Beckett in the Theatre*, Vol. 1 (London: Calder, 1988) [Includes *Waiting for Godot*. Further volumes to come]

+Editions used for this book

# INDEX